BEST-LOVED

KRAFT

PHILADELPHIA

recipes

Publications International, Ltd.

Front cover photography and photography on pages 33, 37, 39, 61, 63, 65, 75, 91, 93, 105, 120, 129, 131, 137, 141, 143, 151, 153, 157, 159, 207, 209, 215, 241, 243, 245, and 247 by Stephen Hamilton Photographics.

Photographers: Tate Hunt, Raymond Barrera
Photographers' Assistants: Chris Gurley, Stevi Savage
Prop Stylist: Tom Hamilton
Food Stylists: Amy Andrews, Kathy Joy
Assistant Food Stylist: Elaine Funk

Pictured on the front cover (clockwise from top): PHILADELPHIA 3-Step White Chocolate Raspberry Swirl Cheesecake *(page 48)*, Cheesy Spinach and Bacon Dip *(page 208)*, OREO No-Bake Cheesecake *(page 100)*, White Chocolate Cheesecake *(page 30)*, PHILADELPHIA No-Bake Chocolate Cherry Cheesecake *(page 108)*, *and* Zesty Chicken Pot Pie *(page 216)*.

Pictured on the back cover (left to right): "Fruit Smoothie" No-Bake Cheesecake *(page 106)*, 20-Minute Skillet Salmon *(page 240)* and Blue Cheese Mushrooms *(page 166)*.

ISBN-13: 978-1-4127-9578-4
ISBN-10: 1-4127-9578-8

Library of Congress Control Number: 2008924185

Manufactured in China.

8 7 6 5 4 3 2 1

Microwave Cooking: Microwave ovens vary in wattage. Use the cooking times as guidelines and check for doneness before adding more time.

Preparation/Cooking Times: Preparation times are based on the approximate amount of time required to assemble the recipe before cooking, baking, chilling, or serving. These times include preparation steps such as measuring, chopping, and mixing. The fact that some preparations and cooking can be done simultaneously is taken into account.

Preparation of optional ingredients and serving suggestions is not included.

For consumer inquiries, call Kraft Foods Consumer Hotline at (800) 431-1001.

contents

8

68

120

cheesecake 101

Follow these simple techniques for cheesecake success

USE Philly. During tests of New York style cheesecake made with **PHILADELPHIA** Cream Cheese versus store brand versions, consumers rated Philly Cheesecake as better tasting.

SET OUT ingredients about 10 minutes before baking. This allows ingredients to come to the same temperature before baking. Cut cream cheese into cubes for faster softening and easier mixing.

USE a 13×9-in. baking pan. Place foil over inverted 13×9-in. pan, leaving about 3 inches of foil extending on short sides of pan. Crease at corners to ensure a wrinkle-free foil liner. Remove foil liner; turn pan over and slip liner into pan. Pour cake mixture into foil-lined pan. Create "handles" by crunching extended foil.

DO NOT over-beat. Over-stirring can add too much air into batter, which can cause cheesecake to crack. Beat in eggs, one at time, on low speed until just blended. Gently stir in flavoring ingredients such as chocolate at the end of mixing process.

PREHEAT oven. While preparing filling, heat oven to recommended temperature. Bake cheesecake on middle rack of oven. Help prevent cheesecake from cracking by baking it in a moist oven. Place a 13×9-in. baking pan half-filled with hot tap water on bottom rack of oven while cheesecake bakes on middle rack.

NO PEEKING! Opening the oven door while cheesecake is baking causes drafts that may lead to cracking. Cheesecake is done if the top is slightly puffy and set except for a small area in the center that should still appear soft and jiggly (about the size of a silver dollar). This will set upon cooling.

LOOSEN IMMEDIATELY to prevent cracking. Immediately run a knife around edge of cheesecake to loosen from sides of pan. Cool cheesecake, away from drafts, for about an hour before refrigerating. Lift up cooked and cooled cheesecake out of baking dish using handles. Place on plate, carefully removing foil from underneath. Decorate as desired.

classic cheesecakes

Timeless favorites everyone will love

PHILLY blueberry swirl cheesecake
(recipe on page 8)

PHILLY blueberry swirl cheesecake

prep: *15 min.*
plus refrigerating

bake: *45 min.*

makes: *16 servings.*

1 cup **HONEY MAID** Graham Cracker Crumbs

1 cup plus 3 Tbsp. sugar, divided

3 Tbsp. butter or margarine, melted

4 pkg. (8 oz. each) **PHILADELPHIA** Cream Cheese, softened

1 tsp. vanilla

1 cup **BREAKSTONE'S** or **KNUDSEN** Sour Cream

4 eggs

2 cups fresh or thawed frozen blueberries

1 Preheat oven to 325°F. Mix crumbs, 3 Tbsp. of the sugar and the butter. Press firmly onto bottom of foil-lined 13×9-inch baking pan. Bake 10 min.

2 Beat cream cheese, remaining 1 cup sugar and the vanilla in large bowl with electric mixer on medium speed until well blended. Add sour cream; mix well. Add eggs, 1 at a time, beating on low speed after each addition just until blended. Pour over crust. Purée the blueberries in a blender or food processor. Gently drop spoonfuls of the puréed blueberries over batter; cut through batter several times with knife for marble effect.

3 Bake 45 min. or until center is almost set; cool. Refrigerate at least 4 hours or overnight. Garnish as desired. Store leftover cheesecake in refrigerator.

classic cheesecakes

chocolate royale cheesecake squares

24 **OREO** Chocolate Sandwich Cookies, crushed (about 2 cups)

¼ cup (½ stick) butter or margarine, melted

4 pkg. (8 oz. each) **PHILADELPHIA** Cream Cheese, softened

1 cup sugar

2 Tbsp. all-purpose flour

1 tsp. vanilla

1 pkg. (8 squares) **BAKER'S** Semi-Sweet Baking Chocolate, melted, slightly cooled

4 eggs

prep: *20 min. plus refrigerating*

bake: *50 min.*

makes: *32 servings, 1 square each.*

1 Preheat oven to 325°F. Mix crumbs and butter; press firmly onto bottom of 13×9-inch baking pan. Bake 10 min.

2 Beat cream cheese, sugar, flour and vanilla in large bowl with electric mixer on medium speed until well blended. Add melted chocolate; mix well. Add eggs, 1 at a time, mixing on low speed after each addition just until blended. Pour over crust.

3 Bake 45 to 50 min. or until center is almost set. Refrigerate at least 4 hours or overnight. Cut into 32 squares to serve. Store leftover dessert squares in refrigerator.

classic cheesecakes

new york cheesecake

jazz it up
Omit pie filling. Arrange 2 cups mixed berries on top of chilled cheesecake. Brush with 2 Tbsp. melted strawberry jelly.

prep: *15 min. plus refrigerating*

bake: *40 min.*

makes: *16 servings, 1 slice each.*

1 cup crushed **HONEY MAID** Honey Grahams (about 6 grahams)

3 Tbsp. sugar

3 Tbsp. butter or margarine, melted

5 pkg. (8 oz. each) **PHILADELPHIA** Cream Cheese, softened

1 cup sugar

3 Tbsp. all-purpose flour

1 Tbsp. vanilla

1 cup **BREAKSTONE'S** or **KNUDSEN** Sour Cream

4 eggs

1 can (21 oz.) cherry pie filling

1 Preheat oven to 325°F. Mix crumbs, 3 Tbsp. of the sugar and butter; press firmly onto bottom of 13×9-inch baking pan. Bake 10 min.

2 Beat cream cheese, 1 cup sugar, flour and vanilla with electric mixer on medium speed until well blended. Add sour cream; mix well. Add eggs, 1 at a time, mixing on low speed after each addition just until blended. Pour over crust.

3 Bake 40 min. or until center is almost set. Cool completely. Refrigerate at least 4 hours or overnight. Top with pie filling before serving. Store leftover cheesecake in refrigerator.

classic cheesecakes

new york-style strawberry swirl cheesecake

substitute
Substitute 1 bag (16 oz.) frozen fruit, thawed, drained and puréed, for the ⅓ cup jam.

healthy living
Save 80 calories, 10 grams of fat and 6 grams of saturated fat per serving by preparing with PHILADELPHIA Neufchâtel Cheese, ⅓ Less Fat than Cream Cheese and BREAKSTONE'S Reduced Fat or KNUDSEN Light Sour Cream (for a delicious 340 calories and 21 grams of fat per serving).

prep: *15 min.*
plus refrigerating

bake: *40 min.*

maks: *16 servings,*
1 slice each.

1 cup **HONEY MAID** Graham Cracker Crumbs

3 Tbsp. sugar

3 Tbsp. butter, melted

5 pkg. (8 oz. each) **PHILADELPHIA** Cream Cheese, softened

1 cup sugar

3 Tbsp. all-purpose flour

1 Tbsp. vanilla

1 cup **BREAKSTONE'S** or **KNUDSEN** Sour Cream

4 eggs

⅓ cup **SMUCKER'S**® Seedless Strawberry Jam

1 Preheat oven to 325°F. Line 13×9-inch baking pan with foil, with ends of foil extending over sides of pan. Mix cracker crumbs, 3 Tbsp. sugar and butter; press firmly onto bottom of prepared pan. Bake 10 min.

2 Beat cream cheese, 1 cup sugar, flour and vanilla in large bowl with electric mixer on medium speed until well blended. Add sour cream; mix well. Add eggs, 1 at a time, mixing on low speed after each addition just until blended. Pour over crust. Gently drop small spoonfuls of jam over batter; cut through batter several times with knife for marble effect.

3 Bake 40 min. or until center is almost set. Cool completely. Refrigerate at least 4 hours or overnight. Lift cheesecake from pan using foil handles. Cut into 16 pieces to serve. Store leftover cheesecake in refrigerator.

SMUCKER'S is a registered trademark owned and licensed by J.M. Smucker Company.

classic cheesecakes

PHILLY brownie cheesecake

prep: *15 min. plus refrigerating*

bake: *40 min.*

makes: *16 servings, 1 piece each.*

1 pkg. (19 to 21 oz.) brownie mix (13×9-inch pan size)

4 pkg. (8 oz. each) **PHILADELPHIA** Cream Cheese, softened

1 cup sugar

1 tsp. vanilla

½ cup **BREAKSTONE'S** or **KNUDSEN** Sour Cream

3 eggs

2 squares **BAKER'S** Semi-Sweet Baking Chocolate

1 Preheat oven to 325°F. Spray 13×9-inch baking pan with cooking spray. Prepare brownie batter as directed on package; pour into prepared pan. Bake 25 min. or until top of brownie is shiny and center is almost set.

2 Meanwhile, beat cream cheese, sugar and vanilla in large bowl with electric mixer on medium speed until well blended. Add sour cream; mix well. Add eggs, 1 at a time, mixing on low speed after each addition just until blended. Gently pour over brownie layer in pan. (Filling will come almost to top of pan.)

3 Bake 40 min. or until center is almost set. Run knife or metal spatula around rim of pan to loosen side of dessert from pan; cool. Refrigerate at least 4 hours or overnight.

4 Melt chocolate as directed on package; drizzle over cheesecake. Refrigerate 15 min. or until chocolate is firm. Cut cheesecake into 16 pieces to serve. Store any leftover cheesecake in refrigerator.

classic cheesecakes

PHILADELPHIA chocolate-vanilla swirl cheesecake

prep: *15 min. plus refrigerating*

bake: *40 min.*

makes: *16 servings, 1 piece each.*

20 **OREO** Chocolate Sandwich Cookies, crushed (about 2 cups)

3 Tbsp. butter, melted

4 pkg. (8 oz. each) **PHILADELPHIA** Cream Cheese, softened

1 cup sugar

1 tsp. vanilla

1 cup **BREAKSTONE'S** or **KNUDSEN** Sour Cream

4 eggs

6 squares **BAKER'S** Semi-Sweet Baking Chocolate, melted, cooled

1 Preheat oven to 325°F. Line 13×9-inch baking pan with foil, with ends of foil extending over sides of pan. Mix cookie crumbs and butter; press firmly onto bottom of prepared pan. Bake 10 min.

2 Beat cream cheese, sugar and vanilla in large bowl with electric mixer on medium speed until well blended. Add sour cream; mix well. Add eggs, 1 at a time, beating on low speed after each addition just until blended. Remove 1 cup of the batter; set aside. Stir melted chocolate into remaining batter in large bowl; pour over crust. Top with spoonfuls of the remaining 1 cup plain batter; cut through batters with knife several times for swirled effect.

3 Bake 40 min. or until center is almost set. Cool. Refrigerate at least 4 hours or overnight. Use foil handles to lift cheesecake from pan before cutting to serve. Garnish as desired. Store leftovers in refrigerator.

classic cheesecakes

caramel-pecan cheesecake bars

prep: *15 min.*
plus refrigerating

bake: *40 min.*

makes: *32 servings,*
1 bar each.

½ cups **NABISCO** Graham Cracker Crumbs

1 cup coarsely chopped **PLANTERS** Pecans, divided

2 Tbsp. granulated sugar

¼ cup (½ stick) butter, melted

4 pkg. (8 oz. each) **PHILADELPHIA** Cream Cheese, softened

1 cup firmly packed brown sugar

2 Tbsp. all-purpose flour

½ cup **BREAKSTONE'S** or **KNUDSEN** Sour Cream

1 Tbsp. vanilla

3 eggs

1 bag (14 oz.) **KRAFT** Caramels, divided

1 Preheat oven to 350°F. Line 13×9-inch baking pan with foil, with ends of foil extending over sides of pan. Mix graham crumbs, ½ cup pecans, granulated sugar and butter; press firmly onto bottom of prepared pan. Bake 10 min.

2 Beat cream cheese, brown sugar and flour in large bowl with electric mixer on medium speed until well blended. Add sour cream and vanilla; mix well. Add eggs, 1 at a time, mixing on low speed after each addition just until blended. Place 36 of the caramels and 1 Tbsp. water in microwaveable bowl. Microwave on HIGH 1 min. or until caramels are completely melted when stirred. Add to cream cheese batter; stir until well blended. Pour over crust.

3 Bake 40 min. or until center is almost set. Sprinkle cheesecake with remaining ½ cup pecans. Refrigerate at least 4 hours or overnight.

4 Place remaining caramels and additional 1 Tbsp. water in microwaveable bowl. Microwave on HIGH 1 min. or until caramels are completely melted when stirred. Drizzle over cheesecake; let stand until set. Remove dessert from pan using foil handles; cut into 32 bars to serve. Store leftover bars in refrigerator.

classic cheesecakes

PHILADELPHIA black
forest cheesecake

prep: *15 min.*
plus refrigerating

bake: *40 min.*

makes: *16 servings,*
1 piece each.

20 **OREO** Chocolate Sandwich Cookies, crushed
(about 2 cups)

3 Tbsp. butter, melted

4 pkg. (8 oz. each) **PHILADELPHIA** Cream Cheese, softened

1 cup sugar

1 tsp. vanilla

1 cup **BREAKSTONE'S** or **KNUDSEN** Sour Cream

6 squares **BAKER'S** Semi-Sweet Baking Chocolate, melted

4 eggs

2 cups thawed **COOL WHIP** Whipped Topping

1 can (21 oz.) cherry pie filling

1 Preheat oven to 325°F. Line 13×9-inch baking pan with foil, with ends of foil extending over sides of pan. Mix cookie crumbs and butter; press firmly onto bottom of prepared pan. Bake 10 min.

2 Beat cream cheese, sugar and vanilla in large bowl with electric mixer on medium speed until well blended. Add sour cream and chocolate; mix well. Add eggs, 1 at a time, mixing on low speed after each addition just until blended. Pour over crust.

3 Bake 40 min. or until center is almost set. Cool. Refrigerate at least 4 hours or overnight. Lift cheesecake from pan, using foil handles. Top with whipped topping and pie filling. Store any leftover cheesecake in refrigerator.

classic cheesecakes

PHILADELPHIA new york cappuccino cheesecake

prep: *15 min.*
plus refrigerating

bake: *1 hour 5 min.*

makes: *16 servings.*

1 cup chocolate wafer cookie crumbs

3 Tbsp. sugar

2 Tbsp. butter or margarine, melted

5 pkg. (8 oz. each) **PHILADELPHIA** Cream Cheese, softened

1 cup sugar

3 Tbsp. all-purpose flour

1 Tbsp. vanilla

3 eggs

1 cup **BREAKSTONE'S** or **KNUDSEN** Sour Cream

1 Tbsp. **MAXWELL HOUSE** Instant Coffee

3 Tbsp. coffee-flavored liqueur

1 Preheat oven to 350°F if using a silver 9-inch springform pan (or to 325°F if using a dark nonstick 9-inch springform pan). Mix crumbs, 3 Tbsp. sugar and the butter; press firmly onto bottom of pan. Bake 10 min.

2 Beat cream cheese, 1 cup sugar, the flour and vanilla in large bowl with electric mixer on medium speed until well blended. Add eggs, 1 at a time, mixing on low speed after each addition just until blended. Add sour cream; mix well. Stir instant coffee granules into liqueur until dissolved. Blend into batter. Pour over crust.

3 Bake 1 hour 5 min. or until center is almost set. Run knife or metal spatula around rim of pan to loosen cake; cool before removing rim of pan. Refrigerate 4 hours or overnight. Store leftover cheesecake in refrigerator.

classic cheesecakes

classic cheesecakes

PHILLY OREO cheesecake

prep: *20 min.*
plus refrigerating

bake: *40 min.*

makes: *16 servings,*
1 piece each.

1 pkg. (1 lb. 2 oz.) **OREO** Chocolate Sandwich Cookies, divided

¼ cup (½ stick) butter or margarine, melted

4 pkg. (8 oz. each) **PHILADELPHIA** Cream Cheese, softened

1 cup sugar

1 tsp. vanilla

1 cup **BREAKSTONE'S** or **KNUDSEN** Sour Cream

4 eggs

1 Preheat oven to 325°F. Line 13×9-inch baking pan with foil, with ends of foil extending over sides of pan. Place 30 of the cookies in food processor; cover. Process 30 to 45 sec. or until finely ground. Add butter; mix well. Press firmly onto bottom of prepared pan.

2 Beat cream cheese, sugar and vanilla in large bowl with electric mixer on medium speed until well blended. Add sour cream; mix well. Add eggs, 1 at a time, beating just until blended after each addition. Chop remaining cookies. Gently stir 1½ cups of the chopped cookies into cream cheese batter. Pour over crust; sprinkle with the remaining chopped cookies.

3 Bake 40 min. or until center is almost set. Cool. Refrigerate 4 hours or overnight. Lift cheesecake from pan, using foil handles. Cut into 16 pieces to serve. Store leftover cheesecake in refrigerator.

classic cheesecakes

chocolate truffle cheesecake

prep: *20 min. plus refrigerating*

bake: *1 hour 5 min.*

makes: *16 servings.*

18 **OREO** Chocolate Sandwich Cookies, finely crushed (about 1½ cups)

2 Tbsp. butter or margarine, melted

3 pkg. (8 oz. each) **PHILADELPHIA** Cream Cheese, softened

1 can (14 oz.) sweetened condensed milk

2 tsp. vanilla

1 pkg. (12 oz.) **BAKER'S** Semi-Sweet Chocolate Chunks, melted, slightly cooled

4 eggs

1 Preheat oven to 300°F if using silver 9-inch springform pan (or to 275°F if using dark nonstick 9-inch springform pan). Mix cookie crumbs and butter; press firmly onto bottom of pan. Set aside.

2 Beat cream cheese, sweetened condensed milk and vanilla in large bowl with electric mixer on medium speed until well blended. Add chocolate; mix well. Add eggs, 1 at a time, mixing on low speed after each addition just until blended. Pour over crust.

3 Bake 1 hour 5 min. or until center is almost set. Run knife or metal spatula around rim of pan to loosen cake; cool before removing rim of pan. Refrigerate at least 4 hours or overnight. Garnish as desired. Store leftover cheesecake in refrigerator.

classic cheesecakes

new york-style sour cream-topped cheesecake

prep: *15 min.*
plus refrigerating

bake: *40 min.*

makes: *16 servings,*
1 piece each.

1½ cups **HONEY MAID** Graham Cracker Crumbs

¼ cup (½ stick) butter, melted

1¼ cups sugar, divided

4 pkg. (8 oz. each) **PHILADELPHIA** Cream Cheese, softened

2 tsp. vanilla, divided

1 container (16 oz.) **BREAKSTONE'S** or **KNUDSEN** Sour Cream, divided

4 eggs

1 Preheat oven to 325°F. Line 13×9-inch baking pan with foil, with ends of foil extending over sides of pan. Mix crumbs, butter and 2 Tbsp. of the sugar; press firmly onto bottom of prepared pan.

2 Beat cream cheese, 1 cup of the remaining sugar and 1 tsp. of the vanilla in large bowl with electric mixer on medium speed until well blended. Add 1 cup of the sour cream; mix well. Add eggs, 1 at a time, beating on low speed after each addition just until blended. Pour over crust.

3 Bake 40 min. or until center is almost set. Mix remaining sour cream, 2 Tbsp. sugar and 1 tsp. vanilla until well blended; carefully spread over cheesecake. Bake an additional 10 min. Cool. Cover; refrigerate 4 hours or overnight. Lift cheesecake from pan, using foil handles. Garnish as desired. Store leftover cheesecake in refrigerator.

classic cheesecakes

white chocolate cheesecake

prep: *30 min.*
plus refrigerating

bake: *1 hour*

makes: *16 servings.*

¾ cup sugar, divided

½ cup (1 stick) butter, softened

1½ tsp. vanilla, divided

1 cup all-purpose flour

4 pkg. (8 oz. each) **PHILADELPHIA** Cream Cheese, softened

2 pkg. (6 squares each) **BAKER'S** Premium White Baking Chocolate, melted, slightly cooled

4 eggs

1 pt. (2 cups) raspberries

1 Preheat oven to 325°F if using a silver 9-inch springform pan (or to 300°F if using a dark nonstick 9-inch springform pan). Beat ¼ cup of the sugar, the butter and ½ tsp. of the vanilla in small bowl with electric mixer on medium speed until light and fluffy. Gradually add flour, mixing on low speed until well blended after each addition. Press firmly onto bottom of pan; prick with fork. Bake 25 min. or until edge is lightly browned.

2 Beat cream cheese, remaining ½ cup sugar and remaining 1 tsp. vanilla in large bowl with electric mixer on medium speed until well blended. Add melted chocolate; mix well. Add eggs, 1 at a time, beating on low speed after each addition just until blended. Pour over crust.

3 Bake 55 min. to 1 hour or until center is almost set. Run knife or metal spatula around rim of pan to loosen cake; cool before removing rim of pan. Refrigerate 4 hours or overnight. Top with the raspberries just before serving. Store leftover cheesecake in refrigerator.

classic cheesecakes

PHILADELPHIA
classic cheesecake

special extra
Top with fresh fruit just before serving.

prep: *20 min.*
plus refrigerating

bake: *55 min.*

makes: *16 servings.*

1½ cups **HONEY MAID** Graham Cracker Crumbs

3 Tbsp. sugar

⅓ cup butter or margarine, melted

4 pkg. (8 oz. each) **PHILADELPHIA** Cream Cheese, softened

1 cup sugar

1 tsp. vanilla

4 eggs

1 Preheat oven to 325°F if using a silver 9-inch springform pan (or to 300°F if using a dark nonstick springform pan). Mix crumbs, 3 Tbsp. sugar and butter; press firmly onto bottom of pan.

2 Beat cream cheese, 1 cup sugar and vanilla with electric mixer on medium speed until well blended. Add eggs, 1 at a time, mixing on low speed after each addition just until blended. Pour over crust.

3 Bake 55 min. or until center is almost set. Loosen cake from side of pan; cool before removing side of pan. Refrigerate 4 hours or overnight. Store leftover cheesecake in refrigerator.

classic cheesecakes

tiramisu cheesecake

prep: *20 min.*
plus refrigerating

bake: *45 min.*

makes: *16 servings,*
1 piece each.

1 box (12 oz.) **NILLA** Wafers (about 88 wafers), divided

5 tsp. **MAXWELL HOUSE** Instant Coffee, divided

3 Tbsp. hot water, divided

4 pkg. (8 oz. each) **PHILADELPHIA** Cream Cheese, softened

1 cup sugar

1 cup **BREAKSTONE'S** or **KNUDSEN** Sour Cream

4 eggs

1 cup thawed **COOL WHIP** Whipped Topping

2 Tbsp. unsweetened cocoa powder

1 Preheat oven to 325°F. Line 13×9-inch baking pan with foil, with ends of foil extending over sides of pan. Layer half of the wafers (about 44) on bottom of prepared pan. Dissolve 2 tsp. of the coffee granules in 2 Tbsp. of the hot water. Brush wafers with half of the dissolved coffee mixture; set remaining aside.

2 Beat cream cheese and sugar in large bowl with electric mixer on medium speed until well blended. Add sour cream; mix well. Add eggs, 1 at a time, mixing on low speed after each addition just until blended. Dissolve remaining 3 tsp. coffee granules in remaining 1 Tbsp. hot water. Remove 3½ cups of the batter; place in medium bowl. Stir in dissolved coffee. Pour coffee-flavored batter over wafers in baking pan. Layer remaining wafers over batter. Brush wafers with reserved dissolved coffee. Pour remaining plain batter over wafers.

3 Bake 45 min. or until center is almost set. Cool. Refrigerate 3 hours or overnight. Lift cheesecake from pan, using foil handles. Spread with whipped topping; sprinkle with cocoa. Cut into 16 pieces to serve. Store leftover cheesecake in refrigerator.

classic cheesecakes

our best chocolate cheesecake

size-wise
Looking for a special treat? One serving of this cheesecake is full of chocolatey flavor.

how to soften cream cheese
Place completely unwrapped pkg. of cream cheese in microwaveable bowl. Microwave on HIGH 45 sec. or until slightly softened.

note
This recipe can also be made in a greased, foil-lined 13×9-inch baking pan. Reduce the baking time by 5 to 10 min.

prep: *30 min. plus refrigerating*

bake: *55 min.*

makes: *16 servings.*

1½ cups crushed **OREO** Chocolate Sandwich Cookies (about 18 cookies)

2 Tbsp. butter or margarine, melted

3 pkg. (8 oz. each) **PHILADELPHIA** Cream Cheese, softened

1 cup sugar

1 tsp. vanilla

1 pkg. (8 squares) **BAKER'S** Semi-Sweet Baking Chocolate, melted, slightly cooled

3 eggs

1 cup thawed **COOL WHIP** Strawberry Whipped Topping

1½ cups assorted seasonal fruit, such as chopped strawberries and sliced kiwi

1 Preheat oven to 325°F if using a silver 9-inch springform pan (or to 300°F if using a dark nonstick 9-inch springform pan). Mix crushed cookies and butter; press firmly onto bottom of pan. Bake 10 min.

2 Beat cream cheese, sugar and vanilla with electric mixer on medium speed until well blended. Add chocolate; mix well. Add eggs, 1 at a time, mixing on low speed after each addition just until blended. Pour over crust.

3 Bake 45 to 55 min. or until center is almost set. Run knife or metal spatula around rim of pan to loosen cake; cool before removing rim of pan. Refrigerate 4 hours or overnight. Top with whipped topping and fruit.

classic cheesecakes

apple pecan cheesecake

jazz it up
For an extra special touch, drizzle KRAFT Caramel Topping over each piece of cheesecake just before serving.

best of season
Take advantage of the many varieties of apples that are available. Try using Jonathan, Granny Smith or Honeycrisp for the topping.

healthy living
Looking for ways to save fat and calories? Save 60 calories and 8 grams of fat per serving by preparing as directed, using PHILADELPHIA Neufchâtel Cheese, ⅓ Less Fat than Cream Cheese and BREAKSTONE'S Reduced Fat or KNUDSEN Light Sour Cream.

prep: *15 min. plus refrigerating*

bake: *55 min.*

makes: *16 servings, 1 piece each.*

1½ cups **HONEY MAID** Graham Cracker Crumbs

¼ cup (½ stick) butter, melted

2 Tbsp. firmly packed brown sugar

4 pkg. (8 oz. each) **PHILADELPHIA** Cream Cheese, softened

1½ cups firmly packed brown sugar, divided

1 tsp. vanilla

1 cup **BREAKSTONE'S** or **KNUDSEN** Sour Cream

4 eggs

4 cups chopped peeled apples (about 3 medium)

¾ cup **PLANTERS** Chopped Pecans

1 tsp. ground cinnamon

1 Preheat oven to 325°F. Line 13×9-inch baking pan with foil, with ends of foil extending over sides of pan. Mix crumbs, butter and 2 Tbsp. brown sugar; press firmly onto bottom of pan.

2 Beat cream cheese, 1 cup of the brown sugar and the vanilla in large bowl with electric mixer on medium speed until well blended. Add sour cream; mix well. Add eggs, 1 at a time, mixing on low speed after each addition just until blended. Pour over crust. Mix remaining ½ cup brown sugar, the apples, pecans and cinnamon; spoon evenly over cheesecake batter.

3 Bake 55 min. or until center is almost set. Cool. Refrigerate 4 hours or overnight. Let stand at room temperature 30 min. before serving. Lift cheesecake from pan, using foil handles. Cut into 16 pieces. Store leftover cheesecake in refrigerator.

classic cheesecakes

fruity cheesecake

prep: *30 min.*
plus refrigerating

bake: *1 hour*

makes: *24 servings.*

1 cup crushed **NILLA** Wafers (about 25 wafers)

3 Tbsp. butter or margarine, melted

3 Tbsp. sugar

4 pkg. (8 oz. each) **PHILADELPHIA** Cream Cheese, softened

1 cup sugar

2 Tbsp. all-purpose flour

1 cup **BREAKSTONE'S** or **KNUDSEN** Sour Cream

4 eggs

1 pkg. (4-serving size) **JELL-O** Lemon Flavor Instant Pudding & Pie Filling

2 cups thawed **COOL WHIP** Strawberry Whipped Topping or **COOL WHIP** Whipped Topping

1 cup each: blueberries, sliced strawberries and peeled sliced kiwi

1 Preheat oven to 325°F. Mix crumbs, butter and 3 Tbsp. sugar; press firmly onto bottom of foil-lined 13×9-inch baking pan. Bake 10 min.

2 Beat cream cheese, 1 cup sugar and the flour in large bowl with electric mixer on medium speed until well blended. Add sour cream; mix well. Add eggs, 1 at a time, mixing on low speed after each addition just until blended. Stir in dry pudding mix. Pour over crust.

3 Bake 1 hour or until center is almost set. Cool in pan on wire rack. Refrigerate 4 hours or overnight. Lift cheesecake out of pan with foil handles; place on serving platter. Spread with the whipped topping; top with fruit.

classic cheesecakes

triple-citrus cheesecake

prep: *30 min.*
plus refrigerating

bake: *1 hour 5 min.*

makes: *16 servings.*

1 cup **HONEY MAID** Graham Cracker Crumbs

⅓ cup firmly packed brown sugar

¼ cup (½ stick) butter or margarine, melted

4 pkg. (8 oz. each) **PHILADELPHIA** Cream Cheese, softened

1 cup granulated sugar

2 Tbsp. all-purpose flour

1 tsp. vanilla

4 eggs

1 Tbsp. fresh lemon juice

1 Tbsp. fresh lime juice

1 Tbsp. fresh orange juice

1 tsp. grated lemon peel

1 tsp. grated lime peel

1 tsp. grated orange peel

1 Preheat oven to 325°F if using a silver 9-inch springform pan (or to 300°F if using a dark nonstick 9-inch springform pan). Mix crumbs, brown sugar and butter; press firmly onto bottom of pan. Bake 10 min.

2 Beat cream cheese, granulated sugar, flour and vanilla with electric mixer on medium speed until well blended. Add eggs, 1 at a time, mixing on low speed after each addition just until blended. Stir in remaining ingredients; pour over crust.

3 Bake 1 hour 5 min. or until center is almost set. Run knife or metal spatula around rim of pan to loosen cake; cool before removing rim of pan. Refrigerate 4 hours or overnight. Garnish as desired. Store leftover cheesecake in refrigerator.

classic cheesecakes

lemon cheesecake

prep: *15 min. plus refrigerating*

bake: *50 min.*

makes: *12 servings.*

1½ cups **HONEY MAID** Graham Cracker Crumbs, finely crushed

1¼ cups sugar, divided

3 Tbsp. butter or margarine, melted

3 pkg. (8 oz. each) **PHILADELPHIA** Cream Cheese, softened

1 cup **BREAKSTONE'S** or **KNUDSEN** Sour Cream

Grated peel and juice from 1 medium lemon

3 eggs

1 Preheat oven to 350°F if using a silver 9-inch springform pan (or to 325°F if using a dark nonstick 9-inch springform pan). Mix crumbs, ¼ cup of the sugar and butter. Reserve ½ cup of the crumb mixture; press remaining crumb mixture firmly onto bottom of pan. Set aside.

2 Beat cream cheese and remaining 1 cup sugar in large bowl with electric mixer on medium speed until well blended. Add sour cream, lemon peel and juice; mix well. Add eggs, 1 at a time, beating on low speed after each addition just until blended. Pour over crust; sprinkle with reserved crumb mixture.

3 Bake 45 to 50 min. or until center is almost set. Turn off oven. Open door slightly; let cheesecake stand in oven 30 min. Remove to wire rack. Run knife or metal spatula around rim of pan to loosen cake; cool before removing rim of pan. Refrigerate at least 4 hours or overnight. Garnish as desired. Store leftover cheesecake in refrigerator.

classic cheesecakes

3-step cheesecakes

Quick and easy desserts

PHILADELPHIA 3-STEP white chocolate
raspberry swirl cheesecake
(recipe on page 48)

PHILADELPHIA 3-STEP
white chocolate raspberry
swirl cheesecake

prep: *10 min.*
plus refrigerating

bake: *40 min.*

makes: *8 servings.*

2 pkg. (8 oz. each) **PHILADELPHIA** Cream Cheese, softened

½ cup sugar

½ tsp. vanilla

2 eggs

3 squares **BAKER'S** Premium White Baking Chocolate, melted

1 **OREO** Pie Crust (6 oz.)

3 Tbsp. raspberry preserves

1 Preheat oven to 350°F. Beat cream cheese, sugar and vanilla with electric mixer on medium speed until well blended. Add eggs; mix just until blended. Stir in white chocolate. Pour into crust.

2 Microwave preserves in small bowl on HIGH 15 sec. or until melted. Dot top of cheesecake with small spoonfuls of preserves. Cut through batter with knife several times for marble effect.

3 Bake 35 to 40 min. or until center is almost set. Cool. Refrigerate 3 hours or overnight. Store leftover cheesecake in refrigerator.

PHILADELPHIA 3-STEP
luscious lemon cheesecake

2 pkg. (8 oz. each) **PHILADELPHIA** Cream Cheese, softened

½ cup sugar

½ tsp. grated lemon peel

1 Tbsp. fresh lemon juice

½ tsp. vanilla

2 eggs

1 **HONEY MAID** Graham Pie Crust (6 oz.)

prep: *10 min.*
plus refrigerating

bake: *40 min.*

makes: *8 servings.*

1 Preheat oven to 350°F. Beat cream cheese, sugar, peel, juice and vanilla with electric mixer on medium speed until well blended. Add eggs; mix just until blended.

2 Pour into crust.

3 Bake 40 min. or until center is almost set. Cool. Refrigerate at least 4 hours. Garnish as desired. Store leftover cheesecake in refrigerator.

PHILADELPHIA 3-STEP
key lime cheesecake

prep: *10 min.*
plus refrigerating

bake: *40 min.*

makes: *8 servings.*

2 pkg. (8 oz. each) **PHILADELPHIA** Cream Cheese, softened

½ cup sugar

1 tsp. grated lime peel

2 Tbsp. fresh lime juice

½ tsp. vanilla

2 eggs

1 **HONEY MAID** Graham Pie Crust (6 oz.)

1 cup thawed **COOL WHIP** Whipped Topping

1 Preheat oven to 350°F. Beat cream cheese, sugar, peel, juice and vanilla with electric mixer on medium speed until well blended. Add eggs; mix just until blended.

2 Pour into crust.

3 Bake 40 min. or until center is almost set. Cool. Refrigerate 3 hours or overnight. Top with whipped topping just before serving. Garnish as desired. Store leftover cheesecake in refrigerator.

3-step cheesecakes

PHILADELPHIA 3-STEP double layer pumpkin cheesecake

prep: *10 min. plus refrigerating*

bake: *40 min.*

makes: *8 servings.*

2 pkg. (8 oz. each) **PHILADELPHIA** Cream Cheese, softened

½ cup sugar

½ tsp. vanilla

2 eggs

½ cup canned pumpkin

½ tsp. ground cinnamon

Dash ground cloves

Dash ground nutmeg

1 **HONEY MAID** Graham Pie Crust (6 oz.)

1 Preheat oven to 325°F. Beat cream cheese, sugar and vanilla with electric mixer on medium speed until well blended. Add eggs, 1 at a time, mixing on low speed after each addition just until blended. Remove 1 cup of the batter; stir in pumpkin and spices.

2 Pour remaining plain batter into crust. Top with pumpkin batter.

3 Bake 40 min. or until center is almost set. Cool. Refrigerate 3 hours or overnight. Garnish as desired. Store leftover cheesecake in refrigerator.

3-step cheesecakes

PHILADELPHIA 3-STEP
double chocolate layer cheesecake

prep: *10 min.*
plus refrigerating

bake: *40 min.*

makes: *8 servings.*

2 pkg. (8 oz. each) **PHILADELPHIA** Cream Cheese, softened

½ cup sugar

½ tsp. vanilla

2 eggs

3 squares **BAKER'S** Semi-Sweet Baking Chocolate, melted, cooled slightly

1 OREO Pie Crust (6 oz.)

½ cup thawed **COOL WHIP** Whipped Topping

4 fresh strawberries, halved

1 Preheat oven to 350°F. Beat cream cheese, sugar and vanilla in large bowl with electric mixer on medium speed until well blended. Add eggs, 1 at a time, beating on low speed after each addition just until blended.

2 Remove 1 cup of the batter to small bowl; stir in melted chocolate. Pour into crust; top with remaining plain batter.

3 Bake 40 min. or until center is almost set. Cool. Refrigerate 3 hours or overnight. Top with whipped topping and strawberries just before serving. Store leftover cheesecake in refrigerator.

3-step cheesecakes

PHILADELPHIA 3-STEP
chocolate chip cheesecake

prep: *10 min.*
plus refrigerating

bake: *40 min.*

makes: *8 servings.*

 2 pkg. (8 oz. each) **PHILADELPHIA** Cream Cheese, softened

½ cup sugar

½ tsp. vanilla

 2 eggs

¾ cup miniature semi-sweet chocolate chips, divided

 1 **HONEY MAID** Graham Pie Crust (6 oz.)

1 Preheat oven to 350°F. Beat cream cheese, sugar and vanilla in large bowl with electric mixer on medium speed until well blended. Add eggs; mix just until blended. Stir in ½ cup of the chips.

2 Pour into crust. Sprinkle with remaining ¼ cup chips.

3 Bake 40 min. or until center is almost set. Cool. Refrigerate 3 hours or overnight. Store leftover cheesecake in refrigerator.

3-step cheesecakes

PHILADELPHIA 3-STEP
coconut cheesecake

prep: *10 min.*
plus refrigerating

bake: *40 min.*

makes: *10 servings.*

2 pkg. (8 oz. each) **PHILADELPHIA** Cream Cheese, softened

½ cup cream of coconut

½ cup sugar

½ tsp. vanilla

2 eggs

1 **HONEY MAID** Graham Pie Crust (6 oz.)

2 cups thawed **COOL WHIP** Whipped Topping

½ cup **BAKER'S ANGEL FLAKE** Coconut, toasted

1 Preheat oven to 350°F. Beat cream cheese, cream of coconut, sugar and vanilla with electric mixer on medium speed until well blended. Add eggs; mix just until blended.

2 Pour into crust.

3 Bake 40 min. or until center is almost set. Cool. Refrigerate 3 hours or overnight. Top with whipped topping and toasted coconut just before serving. Store leftover cheesecake in refrigerator.

3-step cheesecakes

PHILADELPHIA 3-STEP
toffee crunch cheesecake

size it up
Special recipes are fun to eat as part of an annual celebration. Enjoy a serving of this rich and indulgent dessert at your next family gathering.

great substitute
For extra chocolate flavor, substitute 1 OREO Pie Crust (6 oz.) for the graham pie crust.

prep: *10 min.*
plus refrigerating

bake: *40 min.*

makes: *8 servings.*

2 pkg. (8 oz. each) **PHILADELPHIA** Cream Cheese, softened

½ cup firmly packed brown sugar

½ tsp. vanilla

2 eggs

4 chocolate-covered English toffee bars (1.4 oz. each), chopped (about 1 cup), divided

1 **HONEY MAID** Graham Pie Crust (6 oz.)

1 Preheat oven to 350°F. Beat cream cheese, sugar and vanilla in large bowl with electric mixer on medium speed until well blended. Add eggs; mix just until blended. Stir in ¾ cup of the chopped toffee bars.

2 Pour into crust. Sprinkle with remaining chopped toffee bars.

3 Bake 35 to 40 min. or until center is almost set. Cool. Refrigerate 3 hours or overnight. Store leftover cheesecake in refrigerator.

3-step cheesecakes

PHILADELPHIA 3-STEP
cheesecake bars

size it up
Enjoy a serving of this rich and indulgent treat on special occasions.

how to easily remove bars from pan
Line pan with foil before pressing crumb mixture onto bottom of pan.

PHILADELPHIA 3-STEP cheesecake
Omit crumbs and butter. Prepare batter as directed; pour into 1 HONEY MAID Graham Pie Crust (6 oz.). Bake and cool as directed.

prep: *10 min.*
plus refrigerating

bake: *40 min.*

makes: *16 servings, 1 bar each.*

1½ cups **HONEY MAID** Graham Cracker Crumbs

¼ cup (½ stick) butter or margarine, melted

2 pkg. (8 oz. each) **PHILADELPHIA** Cream Cheese, softened

½ cup sugar

½ tsp. vanilla

2 eggs

1 Preheat oven to 350°F. Mix crumbs and butter; press firmly onto bottom of 8- or 9-inch baking pan. Beat cream cheese, sugar and vanilla with electric mixer on medium speed until well blended. Add eggs; mix just until blended. Pour over crust.

2 Bake 40 min. or until center is almost set. Cool.

3 Refrigerate 3 hours or overnight. Cut into 16 bars. Store leftover bars in refrigerator.

3-step cheesecakes

PHILADELPHIA 3-STEP
amaretto berry cheesecake

2 pkg. (8 oz. each) **PHILADELPHIA** Cream Cheese, softened

½ cup sugar

½ tsp. vanilla

3 Tbsp. almond-flavored liqueur

2 eggs

1 **HONEY MAID** Graham Pie Crust (6 oz.)

2 cups mixed berries (blueberries, raspberries and sliced strawberries)

1 Preheat oven to 350°F. Beat cream cheese, sugar and vanilla in large bowl with electric mixer on medium speed until well blended. Add liqueur; mix well. Add eggs; beat just until blended.

2 Pour into crust.

3 Bake 35 to 40 min. or until center is almost set. Cool. Refrigerate 3 hours or overnight. Top with berries just before serving. Store leftover cheesecake in refrigerator.

size it up
This berry cheesecake is the perfect choice for a special occasion. Plan ahead and eat accordingly before indulging in a slice of this cake.

how to soften cream cheese
Place completely unwrapped packages of cream cheese on microwaveable plate. Microwave on HIGH 20 seconds or until slightly softened.

great substitute
Prepare as directed, substituting 1 tsp. almond extract for the almond-flavored liqueur.

prep: *10 min.*
plus refrigerating

bake: *40 min.*

makes: *8 servings.*

celebration treats & cheesecakes

Special sweets for every occasion

white chocolate cherry pecan cheesecake
(recipe on page 68)

white chocolate cherry pecan cheesecake

prep: *30 min. plus refrigerating*

bake: *1 hour.*

makes: *16 servings.*

1 cup **PLANTERS** Pecan Halves, toasted, divided

1½ cups **HONEY MAID** Graham Cracker Crumbs

¼ cup sugar

¼ cup (½ stick) margarine or butter, melted

3 pkg. (8 oz. each) **PHILADELPHIA** Cream Cheese, softened

1 can (14 oz.) sweetened condensed milk

1 pkg. (6 squares) **BAKER'S** Premium White Baking Chocolate, melted

2 tsp. vanilla, divided

4 eggs

1 can (21 oz.) cherry pie filling

1 cup thawed **COOL WHIP** Whipped Topping

1 Preheat oven to 300°F if using a silver 9-inch springform pan (or to 275°F if using a dark nonstick 9-inch springform pan). Reserve 16 of the pecan halves for garnish. Finely chop remaining pecans; mix with graham crumbs, sugar and margarine. Press firmly onto bottom of pan.

2 Beat cream cheese in large bowl with electric mixer on medium speed until creamy. Gradually add sweetened condensed milk, beating until well blended. Add chocolate and 1 tsp. of the vanilla; mix well. Add eggs, 1 at a time, mixing on low speed after each addition just until blended. Pour over crust.

3 Bake 1 hour or until center is almost set. Run knife or metal spatula around rim of pan to loosen cake; cool before removing rim of pan. Refrigerate 4 hours or overnight.

4 Mix pie filling and remaining 1 tsp. vanilla; spoon over cheesecake. Top with whipped topping and reserved pecans. Cut into wedges to serve. Store leftover cheesecake in refrigerator.

pumpkin swirl cheesecake

25 **NABISCO** Ginger Snaps, finely crushed (about 1½ cups)

½ cup finely chopped **PLANTERS** Pecans

¼ cup (½ stick) butter, melted

4 pkg. (8 oz. each) **PHILADELPHIA** Cream Cheese, softened

1 cup sugar, divided

1 tsp. vanilla

4 eggs

1 cup canned pumpkin

1 tsp. ground cinnamon

¼ tsp. ground nutmeg

Dash ground cloves

prep: *20 min. plus refrigerating*

bake: *1 hour 5 min.*

makes: *16 servings, 1 piece each.*

1 Preheat oven to 325°F if using a silver 9-inch springform pan (or to 300°F if using a dark nonstick 9-inch springform pan). Mix ginger snap crumbs, pecans and butter; press onto bottom and 1 inch up side of pan.

2 Beat cream cheese, ¾ cup of the sugar and the vanilla with electric mixer until well blended. Add eggs, 1 at a time, mixing on low speed after each addition just until blended. Remove 1½ cups of the batter; place in small bowl. Stir remaining ¼ cup sugar, the pumpkin and spices into remaining batter. Spoon half of the pumpkin batter into crust; top with spoonfuls of half of the reserved plain batter. Repeat layers. Cut through batters with knife several times for marble effect.

3 Bake 55 min. to 1 hour 5 min. or until center is almost set. (Test doneness by gently shaking the pan. If the cheesecake is done, it will be set except for an approximately 2½-inch area in the center that will be soft and jiggly.) Run knife or metal spatula around rim of pan to loosen cake; cool before removing rim. Refrigerate at least 4 hours or overnight. Store leftovers in refrigerator.

celebration treats & cheesecakes

wave-your-flag cheesecake

prep: *20 min.*
plus refrigerating

makes: *20 servings.*

1 qt. strawberries, divided

1½ cups boiling water

2 pkg. (4-serving size each) **JELL-O** Brand Strawberry Flavor Gelatin

Ice cubes

1 cup cold water

1 pkg. (10.75 oz.) pound cake, cut into 10 slices

2 pkg. (8 oz. each) **PHILADELPHIA** Cream Cheese, softened

¼ cup sugar

1 tub (8 oz.) **COOL WHIP** Whipped Topping, thawed

1 cup blueberries

1 Slice 1 cup of the strawberries; set aside. Halve the remaining 3 cups strawberries; set aside. Stir boiling water into dry gelatin mixes in large bowl at least 2 min. until completely dissolved. Add enough ice to cold water to measure 2 cups. Add to gelatin; stir until ice is completely melted. Refrigerate 5 min. or until gelatin is slightly thickened (consistency of unbeaten egg whites).

2 Meanwhile, line bottom of 13×9-inch dish with cake slices. Add sliced strawberries to thickened gelatin; stir gently. Spoon over cake slices. Refrigerate 4 hours or until set.

3 Beat cream cheese and sugar in large bowl with wire whisk or electric mixer until well blended; gently stir in whipped topping. Spread over gelatin. Arrange strawberry halves on cream cheese mixture to resemble the stripes of a flag. Arrange blueberries on cream cheese mixture for the stars. Store any leftover dessert in refrigerator.

celebration treats & cheesecakes

triple-berry cheesecake tart

prep: *15 min.*
plus refrigerating

makes: *10 servings.*

1¼ cups finely crushed **NILLA** Wafers (about 45 wafers)

¼ cup (½ stick) butter, melted

1 pkg. (8 oz.) **PHILADELPHIA** Cream Cheese, softened

¼ cup sugar

1 cup thawed **COOL WHIP** Whipped Topping

2 cups mixed berries (raspberries, sliced strawberries and blueberries)

¾ cup boiling water

1 pkg. (4-serving size) **JELL-O** Brand Lemon Flavor Gelatin

1 cup ice cubes

1 Mix wafer crumbs and butter in small bowl until well blended. Press onto bottom and up side of 9-inch tart pan. Place in freezer while preparing filling.

2 Beat cream cheese and sugar in large bowl with electric mixer on medium speed until well blended. Gently stir in whipped topping. Spoon into crust; top with berries. Cover and refrigerate.

3 Stir boiling water into dry gelatin mix in medium bowl 2 min. until completely dissolved. Add ice cubes; stir until ice is completely melted. Refrigerate about 15 min. or until slightly thickened (consistency of unbeaten egg whites). Spoon gelatin over fruit in pan. Refrigerate 3 hours.

celebration treats & cheesecakes

PHILADELPHIA 3-STEP
crème de menthe cheesecake

size it up
Enjoy a serving of this rich and indulgent cheesecake on a special occasion.

almond cherry cheesecake
Prepare as directed, substituting 2 Tbsp. almond-flavored liqueur for the crème de menthe and using a HONEY MAID Graham Pie Crust. Top with 1 can (21 oz.) cherry pie filling just before serving.

prep time: *10 min. plus refrigerating*

bake: *40 min.*

makes: *8 servings.*

2 pkg. (8 oz. each) **PHILADELPHIA** Cream Cheese, softened

½ cup granulated sugar

½ tsp. vanilla

2 eggs

4 tsp. green crème de menthe

1 **OREO** Pie Crust (6 oz.)

2 tsp. green cake decorating crystals or colored sugar

1 Preheat oven to 350°F. Beat cream cheese, granulated sugar and vanilla with electric mixer on medium speed until well blended. Add eggs; mix well. Stir in crème de menthe.

2 Pour into crust.

3 Bake 40 min. or until center is almost set. Cool. Refrigerate 3 hours or overnight. Sprinkle with decorating crystals just before serving. Store leftover cheesecake in refrigerator.

celebration treats & cheesecakes

PHILADELPHIA 3-STEP
mini cheesecake baskets

size-wise
These baskets are sure to be a hit at an Easter egg hunt. They are fun to make, and each basket is an easy portion to serve.

how to tint coconut
Place coconut and a few drops green food coloring in small resealable plastic bag. Seal bag. Shake bag gently until coconut is evenly tinted.

variation
Omit NILLA Wafers. Prepare as directed, pouring batter evenly into 12 ready-to-use single-serve graham cracker crumb crusts.

prep pime: *10 min.*

total time: *2 hours 30 min.*

makes: *12 servings.*

 2 pkg. (8 oz. each) **PHILADELPHIA** Cream Cheese, softened

½ cup sugar

½ tsp. vanilla

 2 eggs

12 **NILLA** Wafers

1½ cups **BAKER'S ANGEL FLAKE** Coconut, tinted green

36 small jelly beans

12 pieces shoestring licorice (4 inches each)

1 Preheat oven to 350°F. Beat cream cheese, sugar and vanilla with electric mixer on medium speed until well blended. Add eggs; beat just until blended.

2 Place wafer on bottom of each of 12 paper-lined medium muffin cups. Spoon cream cheese mixture evenly over wafers.

3 Bake 20 min. or until centers are almost set. Cool. Refrigerate at least 2 hours. Top evenly with coconut and jelly beans just before serving. Bend each licorice piece, then insert both ends into each cheesecake to resemble the handle of a basket. Store leftover cheesecakes in refrigerator.

celebration treats & cheesecakes

chocolate bliss cheesecake

size-wise
Sweets can add enjoyment to a balanced diet, but remember to keep tabs on portions.

note
If using a dark nonstick 9-inch springform pan, reduce oven temperature to 300°F.

special extras
Dust entire surface of cooled cheesecake with unsweetened cocoa powder using a wire mesh strainer. Or for a festive Valentine's Day garnish, create a heart-shaped design by topping dusted cheesecake with a heart-shaped stencil and sprinkling with powdered sugar. Or garnish cheesecake with fresh strawberries and raspberries just before serving.

prep: *20 min.*
plus refrigerating

bake: *1 hour.*

makes: *12 servings.*

18 **OREO** Chocolate Sandwich Cookies, finely crushed

2 Tbsp. butter or margarine, melted

3 pkg. (8 oz. each) **PHILADELPHIA** Cream Cheese, softened

¾ cup sugar

1 tsp. vanilla

1 pkg. (8 squares) **BAKER'S** Semi-Sweet Baking Chocolate, melted, cooled slightly

3 eggs

1 Preheat oven to 325°F. Mix crumbs and butter; press onto bottom of 9-inch springform pan.

2 Beat cream cheese, sugar and vanilla in large bowl with electric mixer until well blended. Add chocolate; mix well. Add eggs, 1 at a time, mixing on low speed after each addition just until blended. Pour over crust.

3 Bake 55 min. to 1 hour or until center is almost set. Run knife around rim of pan to loosen cake; cool before removing rim. Refrigerate at least 4 hours. Store leftovers in refrigerator.

celebration treats & cheesecakes

great pumpkin cake

1 pkg. (2-layer) cake mix, any flavor

1 pkg. (8 oz.) **PHILADELPHIA** Cream Cheese, softened

¼ cup (½ stick) butter, softened

4 cups powdered sugar

Few drops each: green, red and yellow food coloring

1 **COMET** Ice Cream Cone

1 Prepare cake batter and bake in 12-cup fluted tube pan as directed on package. Cool in pan 10 min. Invert cake onto wire rack; remove pan. Cool cake completely.

2 Meanwhile, beat cream cheese and butter in medium bowl with electric mixer on medium speed until well blended. Gradually add sugar, beating until well blended after each addition. Remove ½ cup of the frosting; place in small bowl. Add green food coloring; stir until well blended. Spread half of the green frosting onto outside of ice cream cone; set aside. Cover and reserve remaining green frosting for later use.

3 Add red and yellow food colorings to remaining white frosting to tint it orange. Spread onto cake to resemble pumpkin. Invert ice cream cone in hole in top of cake for the pumpkin's stem. Pipe the reserved green frosting in vertical lines down side of cake.

cooking know-how

For a more rounded Great Pumpkin Cake, use a tall 12-cup fluted tube pan. As the cake bakes, it rises and forms a rounded top. When cake is unmolded (upside-down), the bottom of the cake will be rounded. If the cake is baked in a shorter 12-cup fluted tube pan, the resulting cake will be flatter.

fun idea

Place black gumdrops on sheet of waxed paper sprinkled with additional granulated sugar. Use a rolling pin to flatten each gumdrop, turning frequently to coat both sides with sugar. Cut into desired shapes with a sharp knife. Use to decorate frosted cake to resemble a jack-o'-lantern.

prep: *30 min.*

bake: *as directed.*

makes: *24 servings, 1 slice each.*

spider web pumpkin cheesecake

size it up

Looking for a dessert to make for Halloween? This special-occasion dessert is sure to fit the bill since it makes enough to serve a crowd of 16.

make it easy

For easy drizzling, pour melted chocolate into small plastic bag. Snip off a small piece from one of the bottom corners of the bag. Gently squeeze bag to drizzle chocolate over cheesecake as directed.

prep: *15 min.*
plus refrigerating

bake: *55 min.*

makes: *16 servings.*

18 **OREO** Chocolate Sandwich Cookies, finely crushed (about 1½ cups)

 2 Tbsp. butter or margarine, melted

 3 pkg. (8 oz. each) **PHILADELPHIA** Cream Cheese, softened

¾ cup sugar

 1 can (15 oz.) pumpkin

 1 Tbsp. pumpkin pie spice

 3 eggs

 1 cup **BREAKSTONE'S** or **KNUDSEN** Sour Cream

 1 square **BAKER'S** Semi-Sweet Baking Chocolate

 1 tsp. butter or margarine

1 Preheat oven to 350°F if using a silver 9-inch springform pan (or 325°F if using a dark 9-inch nonstick springform pan). Mix cookie crumbs and 2 Tbsp. butter; press firmly onto bottom of pan. Set aside.

2 Beat cream cheese and sugar in large bowl with electric mixer on medium speed until well blended. Add pumpkin and pumpkin pie spice; mix well. Add eggs, 1 at a time, mixing on low speed after each addition just until blended. Pour over crust.

3 Bake 50 to 55 min. or until center is almost set; cool slightly. Carefully spread sour cream over top of cheesecake. Run knife or metal spatula around rim of pan to loosen cake; cool before removing rim of pan.

4 Place chocolate and 1 tsp. butter in small microwaveable bowl. Microwave on MEDIUM 30 sec.; stir until chocolate is completely melted. Drizzle over cheesecake in spiral pattern. Starting at center of cheesecake, pull a toothpick through lines from center of cheesecake to outside edge of cheesecake to resemble a spider's web. Refrigerate 4 hours or overnight. Store leftover cheesecake in refrigerator.

pumpkin spice
frosted snack bars

prep: *20 min.*

bake: *35 min.*

makes: *24 servings, 1 piece each.*

1 pkg. (2-layer size) spice cake mix

1 can (15 oz.) pumpkin

1 cup **MIRACLE WHIP** Dressing

3 eggs

1 pkg. (8 oz.) **PHILADELPHIA** Cream Cheese, softened

¼ cup (½ stick) butter, softened

2 Tbsp. milk

1 tsp. vanilla

1 pkg. (16 oz.) powdered sugar (about 4 cups)

1 Preheat oven to 350°F. Grease 13×9-inch baking pan; set aside. Beat cake mix, pumpkin, dressing and eggs in large bowl with electric mixer on medium speed until well blended. Pour into prepared pan.

2 Bake 32 to 35 min. or until wooden toothpick inserted in center comes out clean. Cool completely in pan on wire rack.

3 Beat cream cheese, butter, milk and vanilla in large bowl with electric mixer on medium speed until well blended. Gradually add sugar, beating after each addition until well blended. Spread over cooled cake. Cut into pieces to serve. Store any leftovers in refrigerator.

celebration treats & cheesecakes

chocolate cream ornament cake

size-wise
You'll know it's a special occasion when you get to enjoy a serving of this festive cake.

easy decorating idea
For fun and easy patterns, place cookie cutters on top of cake and fill in shape with colored sugar.

prep: *20 min.*

bake: *as directed.*

makes: *16 servings, 1 slice each.*

1 pkg. (2-layer size) chocolate cake mix

1 pkg. (4-serving size) **JELL-O** Chocolate Flavor Instant Pudding & Pie Filling

1 pkg. (8 oz.) **PHILADELPHIA** Cream Cheese, softened

1 cup powdered sugar

1½ cups thawed **COOL WHIP** Whipped Topping

1 **COMET** ice cream cone

1 piece red string licorice (2 inches)

Decorating gel

Colored sugar

1 Preheat oven to 350°F. Lightly grease 2 (9-inch) round cake pans. Prepare cake batter as directed on package. Blend in dry pudding mix. Pour evenly into prepared pans.

2 Bake as directed on package. Cool 10 min.; remove from pans to wire racks. Cool completely. Meanwhile, beat cream cheese and powdered sugar in small bowl with electric mixer on medium speed until well blended. Add whipped topping; stir until well blended.

3 Place one of the cake layers on serving plate; spread with one-third of the cream cheese mixture. Cover with remaining cake layer. Spread top and side of cake with remaining cream cheese mixture. Poke two small holes in bottom of ice cream cone; insert ends of licorice into holes leaving small loop at top. Place cone next to cake to resemble ornament hanger. Decorate top of cake with decorating gel and colored sugar as desired. Store in refrigerator.

celebration treats & cheesecakes

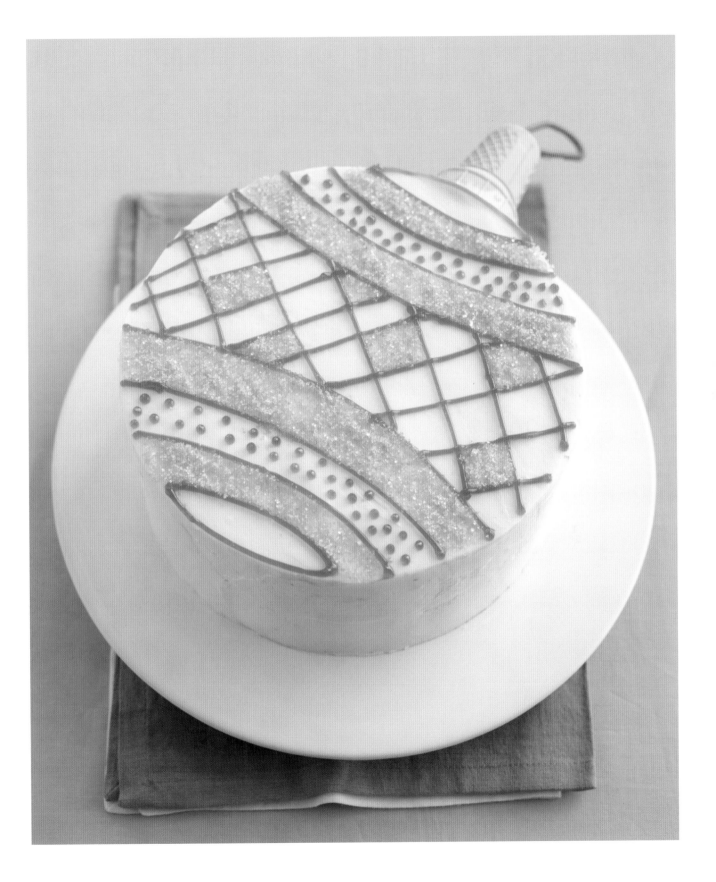

PHILADELPHIA
snowmen cookies

size-wise
A serving of these cookies along with a glass of low-fat milk is sure to be a hit as an after-school snack for your kids.

jazz it up
Decorate with decorating gels, colored sprinkles and nonpareils to resemble snowmen. Cut peanut butter cups in half. Place 1 candy half on top of each snowman for hat.

how to soften cream cheese
Place completely unwrapped package of cream cheese on microwaveable plate. Microwave on HIGH 10 to 15 seconds or until slightly softened.

prep: *20 min.*

bake: *21 min.*

makes: *22 servings, 2 cookies each.*

1 pkg. (8 oz.) **PHILADELPHIA** Cream Cheese, softened

1 cup powdered sugar

¾ cup (1½ sticks) butter or margarine

½ tsp. vanilla

2 cups all-purpose flour

½ tsp. baking soda

Suggested decorations: decorating gels, colored sprinkles, nonpareils and miniature peanut butter cups (optional)

1 Preheat oven to 325°F. Beat cream cheese, sugar, butter and vanilla with electric mixer on medium speed until well blended. Add flour and baking soda; mix well.

2 Shape dough into equal number of ½-inch and 1-inch diameter balls. (You should have about 44 of each size ball.) Using 1 small and 1 large ball for each snowman, place balls, slightly overlapping, on ungreased baking sheet. Flatten to ¼-inch thickness with bottom of glass dipped in additional flour. Repeat with remaining dough.

3 Bake 19 to 21 minutes or until lightly browned. Cool on wire rack. Decorate as desired.

celebration treats & cheesecakes

PHILADELPHIA white chocolate-peppermint cheesecake

serving suggestion
This is a great dessert to share at a holiday party. At 16 servings, there's enough for a crowd.

prep: *15 min. plus refrigerating*

bake: *40 min.*

makes: *16 servings, 1 piece each.*

1½ cups **HONEY MAID** Graham Cracker Crumbs

 3 Tbsp. sugar

¼ cup (½ stick) butter, melted

 4 pkg. (8 oz. each) **PHILADELPHIA** Cream Cheese, softened

 1 cup sugar

¼ tsp. peppermint extract

 1 cup **BREAKSTONE'S** or **KNUDSEN** Sour Cream

 4 squares **BAKER'S** Premium White Baking Chocolate, melted

 4 eggs

 1 cup thawed **COOL WHIP** Whipped Topping

16 starlight mints

1 Preheat oven to 325°F. Line 13×9-inch baking pan with foil, with ends of foil extending over sides of pan. Mix graham cracker crumbs, 3 Tbsp. sugar and the butter; press firmly onto bottom of prepared pan. Bake 10 min.

2 Beat cream cheese, 1 cup sugar and the extract in large bowl with electric mixer on medium speed until well blended. Add sour cream and chocolate; mix well. Add eggs, 1 at a time, mixing on low speed after each addition just until blended. Pour over crust.

3 Bake 40 min. or until center is almost set. Cool. Refrigerate at least 4 hours or overnight. Lift cheesecake from pan, using foil handles. Top each piece with a dollop of the whipped topping and a starlight mint just before serving. Store any leftover cheesecake in refrigerator.

ribbon bar cheesecake

size-wise
This party-size cheesecake is great for large crowds. Be mindful of serving size.

jazz it up
After chocolate topping is firm, place 1 additional chocolate square in microwaveable bowl. Microwave on MEDIUM 1 min., stirring after 30 seconds. Stir until chocolate is completely melted. Pour into small resealable bag; seal bag. Snip off one small corner from bottom of bag; twist top of bag to squeeze chocolate from bag to pipe a special message, such as "Greetings," on top of cheesecake.

prep: *15 min. plus refrigerating*

bake: *40 min.*

makes: *16 servings, 1 square each.*

30 **OREO** Chocolate Sandwich Cookies, crushed

½ cup (1 stick) butter, melted

¼ cup **PLANTERS** Chopped Pecans

¼ cup **BAKER'S ANGEL FLAKE** Coconut

4 pkg. (8 oz. each) **PHILADELPHIA** Cream Cheese, softened

1 cup sugar

4 eggs

½ cup whipping cream

6 squares **BAKER'S** Semi-Sweet Baking Chocolate

1 Preheat oven to 350°F. Mix crushed cookies, butter, pecans and coconut; press firmly onto bottom of 13×9-inch baking pan. Refrigerate while preparing filling.

2 Beat cream cheese and sugar in large bowl with electric mixer on medium speed until well blended. Add eggs, 1 at a time, mixing on low speed after each addition just until blended. Pour over crust.

3 Bake 40 min. or until center is almost set. Cool. Refrigerate 3 hours or overnight. Place whipping cream and chocolate in saucepan. Cook on low heat until chocolate is completely melted and mixture is well blended, stirring occasionally. Pour over cheesecake. Refrigerate 15 min. or until chocolate is firm. Store leftover cheesecake in refrigerator.

celebration treats & cheesecakes

key lime cheesecake pie

prep: *25 min.*
plus refrigerating

bake: *10 min.*

makes: *10 servings.*

1¼ cups finely crushed coconut bar cookies

¼ cup (½ stick) butter or margarine, melted

3 Tbsp. sugar

2 pkg. (8 oz. each) **PHILADELPHIA** Cream Cheese, softened

1 can (14 oz.) sweetened condensed milk

½ tsp. grated lime peel

⅓ cup lime juice

Few drops green food coloring (optional)

1 Preheat oven to 350°F. Mix crumbs, butter and sugar; press firmly onto bottom and up side of 9-inch pie plate. Bake 10 min. Cool.

2 Beat cream cheese and sweetened condensed milk in large bowl with electric mixer on medium speed until well blended. Add peel, juice and food coloring, if desired; mix well. Pour into crust.

3 Refrigerate at least 8 hours or overnight. Store leftover pie in refrigerator.

white chocolate-cranberry cheesecake

prep: *15 min. plus refrigerating*

bake: *50 min.*

makes: *12 servings.*

1¼ cups **OREO** Chocolate Cookie Crumbs

¼ cup (½ stick) butter, melted

3 pkg. (8 oz. each) **PHILADELPHIA** Cream Cheese, softened

¾ cup sugar

3 eggs

4 squares **BAKER'S** Premium White Baking Chocolate, melted

½ cup dried cranberries

1 tsp. grated orange peel

1 Preheat oven to 350°F. Mix crumbs and butter. Press firmly onto bottom of 9-inch springform pan.

2 Beat cream cheese and sugar in large bowl with electric mixer on medium speed until well blended. Add eggs, 1 at a time, mixing just until blended after each addition. Stir in white chocolate, cranberries and orange peel; pour over crust.

3 Bake 45 to 50 min. or until center is almost set if using a silver springform pan. (Or, bake at 325°F for 45 to 50 min. if using a dark nonstick springform pan.) Cool completely. Refrigerate 3 hours or overnight. Garnish with thawed **COOL WHIP** Whipped Topping, orange slices, additional dried cranberries and additional grated white chocolate, if desired.

celebration treats & cheesecakes

no-bake cheesecakes

Oven-free delights

OREO no-bake cheesecake
(recipe on page 100)

OREO no-bake cheesecake

variation
Prepare as directed, using 1 pkg. (18 oz.) Golden Uh-Oh! OREO Chocolate Creme Sandwich Cookies.

prep: *15 min. plus refrigerating*

makes: *24 servings, 1 piece each.*

1 pkg. (1 lb. 2 oz.) **OREO** Chocolate Sandwich Cookies, divided

¼ cup (½ stick) butter, melted

4 pkg. (8 oz. each) **PHILADELPHIA** Cream Cheese, softened

½ cup sugar

1 tsp. vanilla

1 tub (8 oz.) **COOL WHIP** Whipped Topping, thawed

1 Line 13×9-inch pan with foil, with ends of foil extending over sides of pan. Coarsely chop 15 of the cookies; set aside. Finely crush remaining cookies; mix with butter. Press firmly onto bottom of prepared pan. Refrigerate while preparing filling.

2 Beat cream cheese, sugar and vanilla in large bowl with electric mixer on medium speed until well blended. Gently stir in whipped topping and chopped cookies. Spoon over crust; cover.

3 Refrigerate 4 hours or until firm. Store leftover cheesecake in refrigerator.

no-bake cheesecakes

fluffy cheesecake

1 pkg. (8 oz.) **PHILADELPHIA** Cream Cheese, softened

⅓ cup sugar

1 tub (8 oz.) **COOL WHIP** Whipped Topping, thawed

1 **HONEY MAID** Graham Pie Crust (6 oz.)

1 apple, cored, thinly sliced

1 Beat cream cheese and sugar in large bowl with wire whisk or electric mixer until well blended. Gently stir in whipped topping.

2 Spoon into crust.

3 Refrigerate 3 hours or until set. Top with apple slices just before serving.

fluffy cheesecake squares
Omit pie crust. Mix 1 cup HONEY MAID Graham Cracker Crumbs, 2 Tbsp. sugar and ⅓ cup melted butter or margarine. Press onto bottom of foil-lined 8-inch square pan. Continue as directed. Makes 9 servings.

fluffy cherry cheesecake
Prepare and refrigerate as directed. Top with 1½ cups cherry pie filling just before serving.

prep: *15 min. plus refrigerating*

makes: *8 servings.*

no-bake cheesecakes

PHILADELPHIA peaches 'n cream no-bake cheesecake

substitute
Prepare as directed using 1 drained 15-oz. can peaches.

prep: 15 min.
plus refrigerating

makes: 16 servings, 1 piece each.

2 cups **HONEY MAID** Graham Cracker Crumbs

6 Tbsp. margarine, melted

1 cup sugar, divided

4 pkg. (8 oz. each) **PHILADELPHIA** Neufchâtel Cheese, ⅓ Less Fat than Cream Cheese, softened

1 pkg. (4-serving size) **JELL-O** Brand Peach Flavor Gelatin

2 fresh peaches, chopped

1 tub (8 oz.) **COOL WHIP LITE** Whipped Topping, thawed

1 Mix graham crumbs, margarine and ¼ cup of the sugar; press firmly onto bottom of 13×9-inch pan. Refrigerate while preparing filling.

2 Beat Neufchâtel cheese and remaining ¾ cup sugar in large bowl with electric mixer on medium speed until well blended. Add dry gelatin mix; mix until blended. Stir in peaches. Gently stir in whipped topping. Spoon over crust; cover.

3 Refrigerate 4 hours or until firm. Store leftovers in refrigerator.

lem'n berry cheesecake

great substitute
Prepare as directed, using PHILADELPHIA Neufchâtel Cheese, ⅓ Less Fat than Cream Cheese and COOL WHIP LITE Whipped Topping.

prep: *10 min. plus refrigerating*

makes: *8 servings.*

1 pkg. (8 oz.) **PHILADELPHIA** Cream Cheese, softened

¼ cup **COUNTRY TIME** Lemonade Flavor Drink Mix

2 Tbsp. sugar

½ cup milk

2 cups thawed **COOL WHIP** Whipped Topping

1 **HONEY MAID** Graham Pie Crust (6 oz.)

1 cup assorted fresh berries

1 Beat cream cheese, drink mix and sugar in large bowl until well blended. Gradually add milk, mixing until well blended. Gently stir in whipped topping.

2 Spoon into crust.

3 Refrigerate 1 hour or until ready to serve. Garnish with berries.

"fruit smoothie" no-bake cheesecake

2 cups **HONEY MAID** Graham Cracker Crumbs

6 Tbsp. butter, melted

3 Tbsp. sugar

4 pkg. (8 oz. each) **PHILADELPHIA** Neufchâtel Cheese, ⅓ Less Fat than Cream Cheese, softened

¾ cup sugar

1 pkg. (12 oz.) frozen mixed berries (strawberries, raspberries, blueberries and blackberries), thawed, drained

1 tub (8 oz.) **COOL WHIP LITE** Whipped Topping, thawed

1 Line 13×9-inch baking pan with foil, with ends of foil extending over sides of pan. Mix graham crumbs, butter and 3 Tbsp. sugar; press firmly onto bottom of prepared pan. Refrigerate while preparing filling.

2 Beat Neufchâtel cheese and ¾ cup sugar in large bowl with electric mixer on medium speed until well blended. Add drained berries; beat on low speed just until blended. Gently stir in whipped topping. Spoon over crust; cover.

3 Refrigerate 4 hours or until firm. Use foil handles to remove cheesecake from pan before cutting into pieces to serve. Garnish as desired. Store leftover cheesecake in refrigerator.

variation
Omit mixed frozen berries. Add 3 cups fresh mixed berries and additional ¼ cup sugar to Neufchâtel cheese mixture, mixing with electric mixer on medium speed until well blended.

prep: *15 min. plus refrigerating*

makes: *16 servings, 1 piece each.*

no-bake cheesecakes

PHILADELPHIA no-bake chocolate cherry cheesecake

prep: *10 min. plus refrigerating*

makes: *10 servings.*

2 pkg. (8 oz. each) **PHILADELPHIA** Cream Cheese, softened

1 pkg. (4 oz.) **BAKER'S GERMAN'S** Sweet Chocolate, melted, cooled

⅓ cup sugar

1 tub (8 oz.) **COOL WHIP** Whipped Topping, thawed

1 **HONEY MAID** Graham Pie Crust (6 oz.)

1 can (21 oz.) cherry pie filling

1 Beat cream cheese, chocolate and sugar in large bowl with electric mixer on medium speed until well blended. Gently stir in whipped topping.

2 Spoon into crust.

3 Refrigerate 3 hours or overnight. Top with pie filling just before serving. Store leftover cheesecake in refrigerator.

no-bake cheesecakes

chocolate-berry no-bake cheesecake

prep: *15 min.*
plus refrigerating

makes: *10 servings.*

2 squares **BAKER'S** Semi-Sweet Baking Chocolate

2 pkg. (8 oz. each) **PHILADELPHIA** Cream Cheese, softened

⅓ cup sugar

2 cups thawed **COOL WHIP** Chocolate Whipped Topping

1 OREO Pie Crust (6 oz.)

1½ cups quartered strawberries

1 Microwave chocolate in small microwaveable bowl on HIGH 1 min.; stir until chocolate is completely melted. Set aside.

2 Beat cream cheese and sugar in large bowl with electric mixer on medium speed until well blended. Add chocolate; mix well. Gently stir in whipped topping. Spoon into crust.

3 Refrigerate 3 hours or until set. Top with strawberries just before serving. Store leftover cheesecake in refrigerator.

no-bake cheesecakes

PHILADELPHIA blueberry no-bake cheesecake

how to make it with fresh blueberries
Place 2 cups blueberries in small bowl with 2 Tbsp. sugar; mash with fork. Add to Neufchâtel cheese mixture; continue as directed.

prep: *15 min. plus refrigerating*

makes: *16 servings, 1 piece each.*

2 cups **HONEY MAID** Graham Cracker Crumbs

6 Tbsp. margarine, melted

1 cup sugar, divided

4 pkg. (8 oz. each) **PHILADELPHIA** Neufchâtel Cheese, ⅓ Less Fat than Cream Cheese, softened

½ cup blueberry preserves

Grated peel from 1 lemon

1 pkg. (16 oz.) frozen blueberries, thawed, drained

1 tub (8 oz.) **COOL WHIP LITE** Whipped Topping, thawed

1 Mix graham crumbs, margarine and ¼ cup of the sugar; press firmly onto bottom of 13×9-inch pan. Refrigerate while preparing filling.

2 Beat Neufchâtel cheese and remaining ¾ cup sugar in large bowl with electric mixer on medium speed until well blended. Add preserves and lemon peel, mix until blended. Stir in blueberries. Gently stir in whipped topping. Spoon over crust; cover.

3 Refrigerate 4 hours or until firm. Garnish as desired. Store leftovers in refrigerator.

rocky road no-bake cheesecake

prep: *15 min.*
plus refrigerating

makes: *10 servings,*
1 slice each.

3 squares **BAKER'S** Semi-Sweet Baking Chocolate, divided

2 pkg. (8 oz. each) **PHILADELPHIA** Cream Cheese, softened

⅓ cup sugar

¼ cup milk

2 cups thawed **COOL WHIP** Whipped Topping

¾ cup **JET-PUFFED** Miniature Marshmallows

⅓ cup chopped **PLANTERS COCKTAIL** Peanuts

1 **OREO** Pie Crust (6 oz.)

1 Microwave 1 of the chocolate squares in small microwaveable bowl on HIGH 1 min.; stir until chocolate is completely melted. Set aside.

2 Beat cream cheese, sugar and milk in large bowl with electric mixer on medium speed until well blended. Add melted chocolate; mix well. Gently stir in whipped topping, marshmallows and peanuts. Coarsely chop remaining 2 chocolate squares; stir into cream cheese mixture. Spoon into crust.

3 Refrigerate 4 hours or until set. Garnish as desired. Store leftover cheesecake in refrigerator.

no-bake cheesecakes

PHILADELPHIA strawberry fields no-bake cheesecake

how to make it with fresh strawberries
Place 2 cups fresh strawberries in small bowl with additional 2 Tbsp. sugar; mash with fork. Add to Neufchâtel cheese mixture; continue as directed.

prep: *15 min. plus refrigerating*

makes: *16 servings, 1 piece each.*

2 cups **HONEY MAID** Graham Cracker Crumbs

6 Tbsp. margarine, melted

1 cup sugar, divided

4 pkg. (8 oz. each) **PHILADELPHIA** Neufchâtel Cheese, ⅓ Less Fat than Cream Cheese, softened

½ cup strawberry preserves

1 pkg. (16 oz.) frozen strawberries, thawed, drained

1 tub (8 oz.) **COOL WHIP LITE** Whipped Topping, thawed

1 Mix graham crumbs, margarine and ¼ cup of the sugar; press firmly onto bottom of 13×9-inch pan. Refrigerate while preparing filling.

2 Beat Neufchâtel cheese and remaining ¾ cup sugar in large bowl with electric mixer on medium speed until well blended. Add preserves; mix until blended. Stir in strawberries. Gently stir in whipped topping. Spoon over crust; cover.

3 Refrigerate 4 hours or until firm. Store leftovers in refrigerator.

no-bake cheesecakes

everyday desserts

Cupcakes, candy, tarts and more

shortcut carrot cake
(recipe on page 120)

shortcut carrot cake

prep: *30 min.*

bake: *30 min.*

makes: *18 servings.*

1 pkg. (2-layer size) spice cake mix

2 cups shredded carrots (about ½ lb.)

1 can (8 oz.) crushed pineapple, drained

1 cup **PLANTERS** Chopped Pecans, divided

2 pkg. (8 oz. each) **PHILADELPHIA** Cream Cheese, softened

2 cups powdered sugar

1 tub (8 oz.) **COOL WHIP** Whipped Topping, thawed

1 Preheat oven to 350°F. Prepare cake mix batter as directed on package, stirring in carrots, pineapple and ¾ cup of the pecans until well blended. Pour into 2 (9-inch) square baking pans. Bake 25 to 30 min. or until toothpick inserted in centers comes out clean. Cool.

2 Meanwhile, beat cream cheese and sugar with electric mixer or wire whisk until well blended. Stir in whipped topping until well blended.

3 Place 1 cake layer on serving plate. Spread with 1½ cups of the cream cheese mixture. Carefully place second cake layer on top of first cake layer. Frost top and sides of cake with remaining cream cheese mixture. Garnish with remaining ¼ cup pecans. Refrigerate until ready to serve.

everyday desserts

PHILADELPHIA chocolate cheesecakes for two

2 oz. (¼ of 8-oz. pkg.) **PHILADELPHIA** Cream Cheese, softened

1 Tbsp. sugar

1 square **BAKER'S** Semi-Sweet Baking Chocolate, melted

½ cup thawed **COOL WHIP** Whipped Topping

2 **OREO** Chocolate Sandwich Cookies

prep: *10 min.*
plus refrigerating

makes: *2 servings.*

1 Beat cream cheese, sugar and chocolate in medium bowl with wire whisk until well blended. Add whipped topping; mix well.

2 Place 1 cookie on bottom of each of 2 paper-lined medium muffin cups; fill evenly with cream cheese mixture.

3 Refrigerate 2 hours or overnight. (Or, if you are in a hurry, place in the freezer for 1 hour.)

everyday desserts

summer berry trifle

prep: *40 min.*
plus refrigerating

makes: *18 servings.*

1 cup boiling water

1 pkg. (8-serving size) **JELL-O** Brand Strawberry Flavor Gelatin

Ice cubes

½ cup cold water

2 cups mixed berries (raspberries, blueberries, strawberries)

1 pkg. (8 oz.) **PHILADELPHIA** Cream Cheese, softened

1¼ cups cold milk, divided

1 pkg. (4-serving size) **JELL-O** Cheesecake or Vanilla Flavor Instant Pudding & Pie Filling

1 tub (8 oz.) **COOL WHIP** Strawberry Whipped Topping, thawed

1 pkg. (12 oz.) pound cake, cubed

1 Stir boiling water into dry gelatin in large bowl at least 2 min. until completely dissolved. Add enough ice to cold water to measure 1 cup. Add to gelatin; stir until ice is completely melted. Let stand about 15 min. or until thickened. (Spoon drawn through gelatin leaves definite impression.) Stir in berries.

2 Place cream cheese in large bowl; beat with wire whisk until creamy. Gradually add ¼ cup of the milk, beating until well blended. Add remaining 1 cup milk and dry pudding mix; beat 2 min. or until well blended. Gently stir in whipped topping. Set aside.

3 Place about half of the cake cubes in bottom of large serving bowl; cover with half of the pudding mixture. Top with layers of the gelatin mixture, remaining cake cubes and remaining pudding mixture. Refrigerate at least 1 hour. Garnish as desired. Store leftover dessert in refrigerator.

everyday desserts

cafe ladyfinger dessert

shortcut
Substitute 2 tsp.
MAXWELL HOUSE Instant
Coffee, dissolved in 1
cup hot water, for freshly
brewed coffee.

prep: *20 min.*
plus refrigerating

makes: *12 servings.*

2 pkg. (3 oz. each) ladyfingers, split, separated

1 cup freshly brewed strong **MAXWELL HOUSE** Coffee
or **YUBAN** Coffee, any variety, at room temperature,
divided

1 pkg. (8 oz.) **PHILADELPHIA** Fat Free Cream Cheese

2 cups cold fat-free milk

2 pkg. (4-serving size each) **JELL-O** Vanilla Flavor Fat Free
Sugar Free Instant Reduced Calorie Pudding & Pie
Filling

1 tub (8 oz.) **COOL WHIP FREE** Whipped Topping, thawed,
divided

1 Brush cut side of ladyfingers with about ¼ cup of the coffee.
Place ladyfingers on bottom and up side of 2-quart serving bowl.

2 Beat cream cheese and remaining ¾ cup coffee in large bowl
with wire whisk until smooth. Gradually beat in milk until
smooth. Add pudding mixes. Beat with wire whisk until blended.
Gently stir in ½ of the whipped topping. Spoon into prepared
bowl; cover.

3 Refrigerate 1 hour or until ready to serve. Top with remaining
whipped topping.

everyday desserts

tiramisu bowl

prep: *20 min.*
plus refrigerating

makes: *16 servings,
about ⅔ cup each.*

1 pkg. (8 oz.) **PHILADELPHIA** Cream Cheese, softened

3 cups cold milk

2 pkg. (4-serving size each) **JELL-O** Vanilla Flavor Instant Pudding & Pie Filling

1 tub (8 oz.) **COOL WHIP** Whipped Topping, thawed, divided

48 **NILLA** Wafers

½ cup brewed strong **MAXWELL HOUSE** Coffee, cooled

2 squares **BAKER'S** Semi-Sweet Baking Chocolate, coarsely grated

1 cup fresh raspberries

1 Beat cream cheese in large bowl with electric mixer until creamy. Gradually beat in milk. Add dry pudding mixes; mix well. Stir in 2 cups of the whipped topping.

2 Line bottom and sides of a 2½-qt. bowl with half of the wafers; drizzle with half of the coffee. Layer half of the pudding mixture over wafers, and then top with half of the grated chocolate. Repeat all layers starting with the wafers and coffee. Top with remaining whipped topping and raspberries.

3 Refrigerate at least 2 hours. Store leftovers in refrigerator.

everyday desserts

mini OREO surprise cupcakes

size-wise
At 24 servings, these are the perfect sweet treats to serve at your next party.

make it easy
For easy portioning of cream cheese mixture into cake batter, spoon cream cheese mixture into large resealable plastic bag. Seal bag securely. Snip small corner of bag with scissors. Squeeze about 1½ tsp. of the cream cheese mixture over batter in each muffin cup.

prep: *10 min.*

bake: *22 min.*

makes: *24 servings, 1 cupcake each.*

1 pkg. (2-layer size) chocolate cake mix

1 pkg. (8 oz.) **PHILADELPHIA** Cream Cheese, softened

1 egg

2 Tbsp. sugar

48 Mini **OREO** Bite Size Chocolate Sandwich Cookies

1½ cups thawed **COOL WHIP** Whipped Topping

1 Preheat oven to 350°F. Prepare cake batter as directed on package; set aside. Beat cream cheese, egg and sugar until well blended.

2 Spoon cake batter into 24 paper- or foil-lined 2½-inch muffin cups, filling each cup about half full. Top each with about 1½ tsp. of the cream cheese mixture and 1 cookie. Cover evenly with remaining cake batter.

3 Bake 19 to 22 min. or until wooden toothpick inserted in centers comes out clean. Cool 5 min.; remove from pans to wire racks. Cool completely. (There may be an indentation in top of each cupcake after baking.) Top cupcakes with whipped topping and remaining cookies just before serving. Store in tightly covered container in refrigerator up to 3 days.

everyday desserts

PHILADELPHIA
no-bake mini cheesecakes

size-wise
Sweets can add enjoyment to a balanced diet, but remember to keep tabs on portions.

substitute
Substitute miniature chocolate chips for sprinkles.

prep: *10 min.*

makes: *12 servings.*

1 pkg. (8 oz.) **PHILADELPHIA** Cream Cheese, softened

½ cup sugar

1 tub (8 oz.) **COOL WHIP** Whipped Topping, thawed

12 **OREO** Chocolate Sandwich Cookies

Multi-colored sprinkles (optional)

1 Beat cream cheese and sugar until well blended. Gently stir in whipped topping.

2 Place cookies on bottom of 12 paper-lined muffin cups.

3 Spoon cream cheese mixture into muffin cups. Top with multi-colored sprinkles. Refrigerate until ready to serve.

everyday desserts

creamy strawberry cookie "tarts"

prep: *15 min.*
plus refrigerating

makes: *12 servings.*

⅔ cup boiling water

1 pkg. (4-serving size) **JELL-O** Brand Strawberry Flavor Gelatin

1 pkg. (8 oz.) **PHILADELPHIA** Cream Cheese, cubed

1 cup thawed **COOL WHIP** Whipped Topping

12 **CHIPS AHOY!** Real Chocolate Chip Cookies

12 small strawberries

1 Stir boiling water into dry gelatin mix in small bowl at least 2 min. until completely dissolved. Cool 5 min., stirring occasionally.

2 Pour gelatin mixture into blender. Add cream cheese; cover. Blend on medium speed 30 to 45 sec. or until well blended; scrape down side of blender container, if needed. Add whipped topping; cover. Blend on low speed 5 sec. or just until blended.

3 Line 12 muffin pan cups with paper liners; spray with cooking spray. Place 1 cookie on bottom of each prepared cup; top evenly with the gelatin mixture. Refrigerate 1 hour 30 min. or until firm. Top each with a strawberry just before serving. Store leftover desserts in refrigerator.

everyday desserts

CHIPS AHOY!
cheesecake sandwiches

prep: *10 min.*
plus refrigerating

makes: *10 servings,*
1 sandwich each.

4 oz. (½ of 8-oz. pkg.) **PHILADELPHIA** Cream Cheese, softened

2 Tbsp. sugar

1 cup thawed **COOL WHIP** Whipped Topping

20 **CHIPS AHOY!** Real Chocolate Chip Cookies

1 tub (7 oz.) **BAKER'S** Real Milk Dipping Chocolate, melted

1 Beat cream cheese and sugar in large bowl with electric mixer on medium speed until well blended. Stir in whipped topping.

2 Cover bottom (flat) side of each of 10 of the cookies with about 2 Tbsp. of the cream cheese mixture; top each with second cookie, bottom-side down, to form sandwich. Dip half of each sandwich in chocolate; gently shake off excess chocolate. Place in single layer in airtight container.

3 Freeze 3 hours or until firm. Store leftover sandwiches in freezer.

everyday desserts

mini lemon cheesecakes

40 **NILLA** Wafers, finely crushed (about 1⅔ cups crumbs)

¼ cup (½ stick) butter or margarine, softened

3 tsp. grated lemon peel, divided

1 pkg. (8 oz.) **PHILADELPHIA** Cream Cheese, softened

½ cup sugar

1 egg

1 Tbsp. lemon juice

1 Preheat oven to 350°F. Mix wafer crumbs, butter and 2 tsp. of the lemon peel until well blended. Spoon about 2 Tbsp. of the crumb mixture into each of 12 greased or paper-lined medium muffin cups. Press crumb mixture firmly onto bottom and up side of each cup to form crust.

2 Beat cream cheese with electric mixer on medium speed until creamy. Gradually add sugar and remaining 1 tsp. lemon peel, beating after each addition until well blended. Add egg and lemon juice; beat just until blended. Spoon batter evenly into crusts.

3 Bake 40 min. or until lightly browned. Turn oven off. Let cheesecakes stand in oven for 20 min., leaving door slightly ajar. Remove to wire rack to cool. Refrigerate at least 1 hour before serving.

4 Remove from paper liners before serving. Store leftover cheesecakes in refrigerator.

great substitute
Prepare as directed, using PHILADELPHIA Neufchâtel Cheese, ⅓ Less Fat than Cream Cheese.

special extra
Garnish with fresh strawberries and mint sprigs just before serving.

prep: *30 min.*
plus refrigerating

bake: *40 min.*

makes: *12 servings, 1 cheesecake each.*

everyday desserts

strawberry freeze

substitute
Prepare as directed, using
COOL WHIP Strawberry
Whipped Topping.

healthy living
Trim 4 grams of fat and 2
grams of saturated fat per
serving by preparing with
CHIPS AHOY! Reduced
Fat Real Chocolate Chip
Cookies; PHILADELPHIA
Neufchâtel Cheese, ⅓ Less
Fat than Cream Cheese
and COOL WHIP LITE
Whipped Topping.

substitute
Prepare as directed, using
your favorite flavor of
frozen juice or drink
concentrate, such as
raspberry, lemonade,
grape or pink lemonade.

prep: *15 min.*
plus refrigerating

makes: *16 servings.*

12 **CHIPS AHOY!** Real Chocolate Chip Cookies

 1 pkg. (8 oz.) **PHILADELPHIA** Cream Cheese, softened

½ cup sugar

 1 can (12 oz.) frozen berry juice concentrate, thawed

 1 cup crushed strawberries

 1 tub (8 oz.) **COOL WHIP** Whipped Topping, thawed

 2 cups strawberries, halved

1 Arrange cookies in single layer on bottom of 9-inch springform pan; set aside.

2 Beat cream cheese and sugar in large bowl with electric mixer on medium speed until well blended. Gradually add juice concentrate, beating well after each addition. Stir in crushed strawberries. Add whipped topping; stir with wire whisk until well blended. Pour over cookies in pan.

3 Freeze 6 hours or until firm. Remove from freezer; let stand in refrigerator 15 min. to soften slightly. Top with the halved strawberries just before serving. Store leftover dessert in freezer.

everyday desserts

rustic fall fruit tart

size it up
Sweets can add enjoyment to a balanced diet, but choose an appropriate portion.

prep: *15 min.*

bake: *30 min.*

makes: *8 servings.*

1½ cups all-purpose flour

½ cup (1 stick) butter, softened

½ cup (½ of 8-oz. container) **PHILADELPHIA** Cream Cheese Spread

4 medium plums, thinly sliced

2 medium nectarines, thinly sliced

⅓ cup sugar

1 tsp. ground ginger

1 Tbsp. cornstarch

⅓ cup apricot jam

1 Place flour, butter and cream cheese in food processor container; cover. Process, using pulsing action, until mixture is well blended and almost forms a ball. Shape dough into ball; wrap tightly with plastic wrap. Refrigerate 1 hour or until chilled.

2 Preheat oven to 400°F. Place pastry on lightly floured surface; roll out to 12-inch circle. Place on lightly greased baking sheet; set aside. Toss fruit with sugar, ginger and cornstarch. Arrange decoratively over crust to within 2 inches of edge of crust. Fold edge of crust over fruit.

3 Bake 30 min. Remove from oven; spread fruit with jam. Serve warm or at room temperature.

everyday desserts

PHILADELPHIA dessert dip

mallow fruit dip
Add 1 Tbsp. orange juice, 1 tsp. grated orange peel and a dash of ground ginger.

how to soften cream cheese
Place completely unwrapped package of cream cheese on microwaveable plate. Microwave on HIGH 10 to 15 seconds or until slightly softened.

make it easy
To easily remove marshmallow creme from jar, remove lid and seal. Microwave on HIGH 30 seconds.

prep: *5 min.*

makes: *14 servings, 2 Tbsp. each.*

1 pkg. (8 oz.) **PHILADELPHIA** Cream Cheese, softened

1 jar (7 oz.) **JET-PUFFED** Marshmallow Creme

1 Mix ingredients until well blended; cover.

2 Refrigerate until ready to serve.

3 Serve with assorted **NABISCO** Cookies or cut-up fresh fruit.

everyday desserts

cherries in the snow

substitute
Prepare as directed, using PHILADELPHIA Neufchâtel Cheese, ⅓ Less Fat than Cream Cheese and COOL WHIP LITE Whipped Topping.

storage know-how
Once thawed, refrigerate COOL WHIP Whipped Topping for up to 2 weeks or re-freeze.

prep: *10 min.*

makes: *8 servings, about ⅔ cup each.*

1 pkg. (8 oz.) **PHILADELPHIA** Cream Cheese, softened

½ cup sugar

2 cups thawed **COOL WHIP** Whipped Topping

1 can (20 oz.) cherry pie filling, divided

1 Mix cream cheese and sugar until well blended. Stir in whipped topping.

2 Layer heaping 2 Tbsp. cream cheese mixture and 2 Tbsp. pie filling in each of eight stemmed glasses or dessert dishes. Repeat layers.

3 Store leftovers in refrigerator.

everyday desserts

PHILADELPHIA
cherry danish dessert

2 cans (8 oz. each) refrigerated crescent dinner rolls, divided

2 pkg. (8 oz. each) **PHILADELPHIA** Cream Cheese, softened

1½ cups powdered sugar, divided

1 egg white

1 tsp. vanilla

1 can (20 oz.) cherry pie filling

3 Tbsp. milk

1 Preheat oven to 350°F. Unroll 1 of the cans of crescent dough into 2 long rectangles. Place in greased 13×9-inch baking pan; press onto bottom of pan to form crust, firmly pressing seams together to seal.

2 Beat cream cheese, ¾ cup of the sugar, the egg white and vanilla with electric mixer on medium speed until well blended. Spread onto crust; cover with pie filling. Unroll remaining can of crescent dough; separate into 2 long rectangles. Pat out to form 13×9-inch rectangle, pressing seams together to seal. Place over pie filling to form top crust.

3 Bake 25 to 30 min. or until golden brown; cool slightly. Gradually add milk to remaining ¾ cup sugar, beating with wire whisk until well blended. Drizzle over warm dessert. Cut into 24 rectangles to serve. Store leftover dessert in refrigerator.

everyday desserts

chocolate & peanut butter ribbon dessert

size-wise
Savor a serving of this indulgent special-occasion dessert. One loaf makes enough for 12 servings.

how to double the recipe
Line 13×9-inch pan with foil, with ends of foil extending over sides of pan; set aside. Prepare recipe as directed, using the 1 tub (12 oz.) whipped topping but increasing the vanilla to 1 Tbsp. and doubling all remaining ingredients. Do not invert dessert to remove from pan but lift dessert from pan using foil handles. Cut into bars to serve. Makes 24 servings, 1 bar each.

prep: *15 min.*
plus refrigerating

makes: *12 servings.*

12 **NUTTER BUTTER** Peanut Butter Sandwich Cookies, divided

 2 Tbsp. butter, melted

 1 pkg. (8 oz.) **PHILADELPHIA** Cream Cheese, softened

 ½ cup creamy peanut butter

 ½ cup sugar

 2 tsp. vanilla

 1 tub (12 oz.) **COOL WHIP** Whipped Topping, thawed, divided

 2 squares **BAKER'S** Semi-Sweet Baking Chocolate, melted

1 Crush 8 of the cookies in resealable plastic bag with rolling pin. Mix cookie crumbs and butter. Press onto bottom of foil-lined 9×5-inch loaf pan.

2 Mix cream cheese, peanut butter, sugar and vanilla with electric mixer on medium speed until well blended. Gently stir in 3 cups of the whipped topping. Spoon ½ cup of the cream cheese mixture into small bowl. Stir in melted chocolate until well blended; set aside. Spoon half of the remaining cream cheese mixture over crust. Top evenly with chocolate mixture; cover with remaining cream cheese mixture.

3 Freeze 4 hours or overnight until firm. Invert onto plate. Remove foil, then re-invert onto serving platter so that crumb layer is on bottom. Coarsely break the remaining 4 cookies. Top dessert with remaining whipping topping and cookies.

everyday desserts

easy chocolate truffles

size-wise

Put these truffles in pretty fluted candy cups and display on a silver platter for an elegant presentation. Each one is a very special treat. Enjoy a serving after dinner with a cup of freshly brewed coffee.

easy spirited chocolate truffles

Prepare as directed except omit vanilla. Divide truffle mixture into thirds. Add 1 Tbsp. liqueur (almond, coffee or orange-flavored) to each third of mixture; mix well.

prep: *30 min. plus refrigerating*

makes: *24 servings, 3 truffles each.*

1 pkg. (8 oz.) **PHILADELPHIA** Cream Cheese, softened

3 cups powdered sugar

1½ pkg. (12 squares) **BAKER'S** Semi-Sweet Baking Chocolate, melted

1½ tsp. vanilla

Suggested coatings: ground **PLANTERS** Walnuts, unsweetened cocoa, powdered sugar and/or **BAKER'S ANGEL FLAKE** Coconut

1 Beat cream cheese in large bowl with electric mixer on medium speed until smooth. Gradually add sugar, mixing until well blended.

2 Add melted chocolate and vanilla; mix well. Refrigerate 1 hour or until chilled.

3 Shape into 1-inch balls. Roll in walnuts, cocoa, powdered sugar or coconut. Store in refrigerator.

everyday desserts

red velvet cake

prep: *10 min.*

bake: *as directed.*

makes: *16 servings.*

1 pkg. (2-layer size) white cake mix

2 squares **BAKER'S** Unsweetened Baking Chocolate, melted

1 Tbsp. red food coloring

1 pkg. (8 oz.) **PHILADELPHIA** Cream Cheese, softened

½ cup (1 stick) butter or margarine, melted

1 pkg. (16 oz.) powdered sugar (about 4 cups)

½ cup chopped **PLANTERS** Pecans

1 Prepare and bake cake mix as directed on package for 2 (9-inch) round cake layers, adding chocolate and food coloring with water, eggs and oil; cool completely.

2 Beat cream cheese and butter with electric mixer on medium speed until well blended. Gradually add sugar, beating well after each addition. Stir in pecans.

3 Fill and frost cake layers with cream cheese frosting.

everyday desserts

creamy lemon nut bars

substitute
Prepare as directed, using lime juice and grated lime peel.

prep: 15 min.

bake: 30 min.

makes: 32 servings, 1 bar each.

½ cup (1 stick) butter or margarine, softened

⅓ cup powdered sugar

2 tsp. vanilla

1¾ cups all-purpose flour, divided

⅓ cup **PLANTERS** Pecans, chopped

1 pkg. (8 oz.) **PHILADELPHIA** Cream Cheese, softened

2 cups granulated sugar

3 eggs

½ cup lemon juice

1 Tbsp. grated lemon peel

1 Tbsp. powdered sugar

1 Preheat oven to 350°F. Line 13×9-inch baking pan with foil; spray with cooking spray. Mix butter, powdered sugar and vanilla in large bowl. Gradually stir in 1½ cups of the flour and pecans. Press dough firmly onto bottom of prepared pan. Bake 15 min.

2 Beat cream cheese and granulated sugar in medium bowl with electric mixer on high speed until well blended. Add remaining ¼ cup flour and eggs; beat until blended.

3 Stir in lemon juice and peel. Pour over baked crust in pan. Bake 30 min. or until set. Remove from oven; cool completely. Sprinkle with 1 Tbsp. powdered sugar; cut into 32 bars.

everyday desserts

lemon-cream cheese cupcakes

substitute
Prepare as directed, using PHILADELPHIA Neufchâtel Cheese, ⅓ Less Fat than Cream Cheese.

jazz it up
Stir 1 tsp. grated lemon peel into frosting mixture.

prep: *10 min.*

bake: *24 min.*

makes: *24 servings, 1 cupcake each.*

1 pkg. (2-layer size) white cake mix

1 pkg. (4-serving) **JELL-O** Lemon Flavor Instant Pudding & Pie Filling

1 cup water

4 egg whites

2 Tbsp. oil

1 pkg. (16 oz.) powdered sugar

1 pkg. (8 oz.) **PHILADELPHIA** Cream Cheese, softened

¼ cup (½ stick) butter, softened

2 Tbsp. lemon juice

1 Preheat oven to 350°F. Beat cake mix, dry pudding mix, water, egg whites and oil in large bowl with electric mixer on low speed until moistened. (Batter will be thick.) Beat on medium speed 2 min. Spoon batter evenly into 24 paper-lined 2½-inch muffin cups.

2 Bake 21 to 24 min. or until wooden toothpick inserted in centers comes out clean. Cool in pans 10 min.; remove to wire racks. Cool completely.

3 Meanwhile, beat sugar, cream cheese, butter and juice with electric mixer on low speed until well blended. Frost cupcakes.

everyday desserts

cookies & cream freeze

prep: *30 min.*
plus refrigerating

makes: *12 servings, 1 piece each.*

  4 squares **BAKER'S** Semi-Sweet Baking Chocolate

14 **OREO** Chocolate Sandwich Cookies, divided

  1 pkg. (8 oz.) **PHILADELPHIA** Cream Cheese, softened

  ¼ cup sugar

  ½ tsp. vanilla

  1 tub (8 oz.) **COOL WHIP** Whipped Topping, thawed

1 Melt chocolate as directed on package; set aside until ready to use. Line 8½×4½-inch loaf pan with foil, with ends of foil extending over sides of pan. Arrange 8 of the cookies evenly on bottom of pan. Crumble remaining 6 cookies; set aside.

2 Beat cream cheese, sugar and vanilla in medium bowl with electric mixer until well blended. Stir in whipped topping. Remove about 1½ cups of the cream cheese mixture; place in medium bowl. Stir in melted chocolate.

3 Spread remaining cream cheese mixture over cookies in pan; sprinkle with crumbled cookies. Gently press cookies into cream cheese mixture with back of spoon; top with chocolate mixture. Cover. Freeze 3 hours or until firm. Remove from freezer about 15 min. before serving; invert onto serving plate. Peel off foil; let stand at room temperature to soften slightly before cutting to serve.

everyday desserts

banana pudding squares

35 Reduced Fat **NILLA** Wafers, finely crushed

¼ cup (½ stick) margarine, melted

1 pkg. (8 oz.) **PHILADELPHIA** Neufchâtel Cheese, ⅓ Less Fat than Cream Cheese, softened

½ cup powdered sugar

1 tub (8 oz.) **COOL WHIP** Sugar Free Whipped Topping, thawed, divided

3 bananas

3 cups cold fat-free milk

2 pkg. (4-serving size each) **JELL-O** Vanilla Flavor Fat Free Sugar Free Instant Reduced Calorie Pudding & Pie Filling

½ square **BAKER'S** Semi-Sweet Baking Chocolate, grated

1 Combine wafer crumbs and margarine; press onto bottom of 13×9-inch dish. Refrigerate while preparing filling.

2 Mix Neufchâtel cheese and sugar in medium bowl until well blended. Stir in 1½ cups of the whipped topping; spread carefully onto crust. Set aside. Cut bananas crosswise in half, then cut each piece lengthwise in half. Arrange over Neufchâtel cheese mixture.

3 Pour milk into large bowl. Add dry pudding mixes. Beat with wire whisk 2 min. Spoon over bananas. Spread with remaining whipped topping; sprinkle with chocolate. Refrigerate at least 3 hours before serving. Store leftovers in refrigerator.

how to evenly spread whipped topping over dessert
Stir remaining whipped topping gently in tub to soften. Place small dollops of topping evenly over top of dessert, then use a small metal spatula to spread whipped topping in an even layer.

how to easily remove dessert from dish
Line dish with foil before using, with ends of foil extending over sides of dish. Prepare recipe as directed. When ready to serve, remove dessert from dish using foil handles. Cut into pieces to serve.

prep: *30 min. plus refrigerating*

makes: *24 servings.*

everyday desserts

dips & appetizers

Perfect party starters

PHILLY tomato-basil dip
(recipe on page 164)

PHILLY tomato-basil dip

prep: *10 min.*

makes: *1¾ cups or 14 servings, 2 Tbsp. each.*

1 pkg. (8 oz.) **PHILADELPHIA** Neufchâtel Cheese, ⅓ Less Fat than Cream Cheese, softened

2 plum tomatoes, chopped

2 Tbsp. **KRAFT** Zesty Italian Dressing

2 Tbsp. **KRAFT** Shredded Parmesan Cheese

1 Tbsp. finely chopped fresh basil

1 Spread Neufchâtel cheese onto bottom of 9-inch pie plate.

2 Mix tomatoes and dressing; spoon over Neufchâtel cheese. Sprinkle with Parmesan cheese and basil.

3 Serve with **WHEAT THINS** Snack Crackers or assorted cut-up fresh vegetables.

dips & appetizers

PHILLY cheesy pizza dip

1 pkg. (8 oz.) **PHILADELPHIA** Cream Cheese, softened

½ cup pizza sauce

½ cup **KRAFT** Shredded Mozzarella Cheese

2 Tbsp. **KRAFT** 100% Grated Parmesan Cheese

2 Tbsp. each: chopped red and green bell peppers

1 tsp. Italian seasoning

   RITZ Crackers

prep: *10 min.*

makes: *2 cups dip or 16 servings, 2 Tbsp. dip and 5 crackers each.*

1 Spread cream cheese onto bottom of microwaveable 9-inch pie plate. Cover with pizza sauce; top with all remaining ingredients except crackers.

2 Microwave on HIGH 2 min. or until heated through.

3 Serve with the crackers.

blue cheese mushrooms

prep: *30 min.*

broil: *3 min.*

makes: *2 dozen or 24 servings, 1 mushroom each.*

24 medium fresh mushrooms (1 lb.)

¼ cup sliced green onions

1 Tbsp. butter or margarine

1 pkg. (4 oz.) **ATHENOS** Crumbled Blue Cheese

3 oz. **PHILADELPHIA** Cream Cheese, softened

1 Preheat broiler. Remove stems from mushrooms; chop stems. Cook and stir stems and onions in butter in small skillet on medium heat until tender.

2 Add blue cheese and cream cheese; mix well. Spoon evenly into mushroom caps; place on rack of broiler pan.

3 Broil 2 to 3 min. or until golden brown. Serve warm.

PHILLY cheesy chili dip

prep: *5 min.*

makes: *3 cups or 24 servings, 2 Tbsp. each.*

1 pkg. (8 oz.) **PHILADELPHIA** Cream Cheese, softened

1 can (15 oz.) chili

½ cup **KRAFT** Shredded Cheddar Cheese

2 Tbsp. chopped cilantro

1 Spread cream cheese onto bottom of microwaveable pie plate; top with chili and Cheddar cheese.

2 Microwave on HIGH 45 sec. to 1 min. or until Cheddar cheese is melted. Sprinkle with cilantro.

3 Serve with assorted **NABISCO** Crackers.

dips & appetizers

PHILLY shrimp cocktail dip

prep: *10 min.*

makes: *3 cups or 24 servings, 2 Tbsp. each.*

1 pkg. (8 oz.) **PHILADELPHIA** Cream Cheese, softened

¾ lb. cooked shrimp, chopped (about 2 cups)

¾ cup **KRAFT** Cocktail Sauce

¼ cup **KRAFT** Shredded Parmesan Cheese

¼ cup sliced green onions

1 Spread cream cheese onto bottom of 9-inch pie plate. Toss shrimp with cocktail sauce; spoon over cream cheese.

2 Sprinkle with Parmesan cheese and onions.

3 Serve with **WHEAT THINS** Snack Crackers.

dips & appetizers

PHILLY buffalo chicken dip

prep: *10 min.*

makes: *2¼ cups or 18 servings, 2 Tbsp. each.*

1 pkg. (8 oz.) **PHILADELPHIA** Cream Cheese, softened

1 pkg. (6 oz.) **OSCAR MAYER** Oven Roasted Chicken Breast Cuts

½ cup Buffalo wing sauce

¼ cup **KRAFT** Natural Blue Cheese Crumbles

¼ cup sliced green onions

1 Spread cream cheese onto bottom of microwaveable 9-inch pie plate. Mix chicken and sauce; spoon over cream cheese. Sprinkle with blue cheese and onions.

2 Microwave on HIGH 2 min. or until heated through.

3 Serve warm with celery sticks and **WHEAT THINS** Snack Crackers.

dips & appetizers

PHILADELPHIA mexican dip

prep: *10 min.*

makes: *1⅔ cups dip or 13 servings, 2 Tbsp. dip and 16 crackers each.*

1 pkg. (8 oz.) **PHILADELPHIA** Neufchâtel Cheese, ⅓ Less Fat than Cream Cheese, softened

½ cup **TACO BELL**® **HOME ORIGINALS**® Thick 'N Chunky Salsa

½ cup **KRAFT** 2% Milk Shredded Reduced Fat Cheddar Cheese

2 green onions, sliced (about ¼ cup)

WHEAT THINS Reduced Fat Baked Snack Crackers

1 Spread Neufchâtel cheese onto bottom of 9-inch pie plate.

2 Top with layers of salsa, Cheddar cheese and onions.

3 Serve with the crackers.

TACO BELL® and HOME ORIGINALS® are trademarks owned and licensed by Taco Bell Corp.

dips & appetizers

PHILADELPHIA garden vegetable dip

prep: *10 min. plus refrigerating*

makes: *20 servings, 2 Tbsp. each.*

2 pkg. (8 oz. each) **PHILADELPHIA** Cream Cheese, softened

½ cup **KRAFT** Blue Cheese Dressing

½ cup finely chopped broccoli

1 medium carrot, shredded

1 Mix cream cheese and dressing until well blended. Stir in vegetables; cover.

2 Refrigerate several hours or until chilled.

3 Serve with assorted cut-up fresh vegetables.

dips & appetizers

BLT dip

prep: *15 min.*

makes: *2 cups or 16 servings, 2 Tbsp. each.*

1 pkg. (8 oz.) **PHILADELPHIA** Cream Cheese, softened

¾ cup shredded or chopped romaine lettuce

2 plum tomatoes, seeded, chopped

4 slices **OSCAR MAYER** Bacon, crisply cooked, drained and crumbled

1 Spread cream cheese onto bottom of 9-inch pie plate.

2 Top with lettuce and tomatoes; sprinkle with bacon.

3 Serve with **WHEAT THINS** Snack Crackers or assorted cut-up fresh vegetables.

dips & appetizers

savory bruschetta

prep: *15 min.*

bake: *10 min.*

makes: *2 dozen or 24 servings, 1 slice each.*

¼ cup olive oil

1 clove garlic, minced

1 loaf (1 lb.) French bread, cut in half lengthwise

1 pkg. (8 oz.) **PHILADELPHIA** Cream Cheese, softened

3 Tbsp. **KRAFT** 100% Grated Parmesan Cheese

2 Tbsp. chopped pitted ripe olives

1 cup chopped plum tomatoes

¼ cup chopped fresh basil

1 Preheat oven to 400°F. Mix oil and garlic; spread onto cut surfaces of bread. Bake 8 to 10 min. or until lightly browned. Cool.

2 Mix cream cheese and Parmesan cheese with electric mixer on medium speed until blended. Stir in olives.

3 Spread toasted bread halves with cream cheese mixture; top with tomatoes. Cut into 24 slices to serve. Sprinkle with basil.

dips & appetizers

baked crab rangoon

prep: *20 min.*

bake: *20 min.*

makes: *12 servings, 1 wonton each.*

1 can (6 oz.) white crabmeat, drained, flaked

4 oz. (½ of 8-oz. pkg.) **PHILADELPHIA** Neufchâtel Cheese, ⅓ Less Fat than Cream Cheese, softened

¼ cup thinly sliced green onions

¼ cup **KRAFT** Mayo Light Mayonnaise

12 wonton wrappers

1 Preheat oven to 350°F. Mix crabmeat, Neufchâtel cheese, onions and mayo.

2 Spray 12 medium muffin cups with cooking spray. Gently place 1 wonton wrapper in each cup, allowing edges of wrappers to extend above sides of cups. Fill evenly with crabmeat mixture.

3 Bake 18 to 20 min. or until edges are golden brown and filling is heated through. Serve warm. Garnish as desired.

dips & appetizers

cream cheese bacon crescents

prep: *15 min.*

bake: *15 min.*

makes: *16 servings,*
2 crescents each.

1 tub (8 oz.) **PHILADELPHIA** Chive & Onion Light Cream
   Cheese Spread

3 slices **OSCAR MAYER** Bacon, cooked, crumbled

2 cans (8 oz. each) reduced fat refrigerated crescent
   dinner rolls

1 Preheat oven to 375°F. Mix cream cheese spread and bacon in small bowl until well blended.

2 Separate each can of dough into 8 triangles each. Cut each triangle in half lengthwise. Spread each dough triangle with 1 generous tsp. cream cheese mixture. Roll up, starting at shortest side of triangle and rolling to opposite point. Place, point sides down, on ungreased baking sheet.

3 Bake 12 to 15 min. or until golden brown. Serve warm.

dips & appetizers

three pepper quesadillas

prep: *20 min.*

bake: *10 min.*

makes: *30 servings, 1 piece each.*

1 cup thin green bell pepper strips

1 cup thin red bell pepper strips

1 cup thin yellow bell pepper strips

½ cup thin onion slices

⅓ cup butter or margarine

½ tsp. ground cumin

1 pkg. (8 oz.) **PHILADELPHIA** Cream Cheese, softened

1 pkg. (8 oz.) **KRAFT** Shredded Sharp Cheddar Cheese

10 **TACO BELL**® **HOME ORIGINALS**® Flour Tortillas

1 jar (16 oz.) **TACO BELL**® **HOME ORIGINALS**® Thick 'N Chunky Salsa

1 Preheat oven to 425°F. Cook and stir peppers and onion in butter in large skillet on medium-high heat until crisp-tender. Stir in cumin. Drain, reserving liquid.

2 Beat cream cheese and Cheddar cheese with electric mixer on medium speed until well blended. Spoon 2 Tbsp. cheese mixture onto each tortilla; top each evenly with pepper mixture. Fold tortillas in half; place on ungreased baking sheet. Brush with reserved liquid.

3 Bake 10 min. or until heated through. Cut each tortilla into thirds. Serve warm with salsa.

TACO BELL® and HOME ORIGINALS® are trademarks owned and licensed by Taco Bell Corp.

dips & appetizers

barbecue bacon party spread

prep: *15 min.*

makes: *35 servings, 2 Tbsp. spread and 11 Thin Crisps each.*

2 pkg. (8 oz. each) **PHILADELPHIA** Cream Cheese, softened

½ cup **KRAFT THICK 'N SPICY** Original Barbecue Sauce

1 pkg. (2.8 oz.) **OSCAR MAYER** Real Bacon Recipe Pieces

1 small tomato, chopped

½ cup chopped green bell pepper

⅓ cup sliced green onions

1½ cups **KRAFT** Shredded Cheddar Cheese

 TRISCUIT Thin Crisps

1 Spread cream cheese on large platter; drizzle with barbecue sauce.

2 Top with all remaining ingredients except the Thin Crisps.

3 Serve with the Thin Crisps.

dips & appetizers

cool veggie pizza appetizer

prep: *20 min.*
plus refrigerating

bake: *13 min.*

makes: *32 servings.*

2 cans (8 oz. each) refrigerated crescent dinner rolls

1 pkg. (8 oz.) **PHILADELPHIA** Cream Cheese, softened

½ cup **MIRACLE WHIP** Dressing

1 tsp. dill weed

½ tsp. onion salt

1 cup broccoli florets

1 cup chopped green bell pepper

1 cup chopped seeded tomato

¼ cup chopped red onion

1 Preheat oven to 375°F. Separate dough into 4 rectangles. Press onto bottom and up side of 15×10×1-inch baking pan to form crust.

2 Bake 11 to 13 min. or until golden brown; cool.

3 Mix cream cheese, dressing, dill and onion salt until well blended. Spread over crust; top with remaining ingredients. Refrigerate. Cut into squares.

dips & appetizers

PHILLY fresh mediterranean dip

prep: *10 min.*

makes: *1¾ cups or 14 servings, 2 Tbsp. each.*

1 pkg. (8 oz.) **PHILADELPHIA** Neufchâtel Cheese, ⅓ Less Fat than Cream Cheese, softened

½ cup chopped tomato

½ cup chopped cucumbers

½ cup chopped spinach leaves

¼ cup chopped red onions

2 Tbsp. **KRAFT** Greek Vinaigrette Dressing

¼ cup **ATHENOS** Crumbled Feta Cheese with Basil & Tomato

1 Spread Neufchâtel cheese onto bottom of 9-inch pie plate.

2 Mix remaining ingredients except feta cheese; spoon over Neufchâtel cheese. Sprinkle with feta cheese.

3 Serve with **WHEAT THINS** Snack Crackers or assorted cut-up fresh vegetables.

dips & appetizers

PHILLY BBQ ranch chicken dip

prep: *10 min.*

makes: *2¼ cups or 18 servings, 2 Tbsp. each.*

1 pkg. (8 oz.) **PHILADELPHIA** Neufchâtel Cheese, ⅓ Less Fat than Cream Cheese, softened

¼ cup **KRAFT** Barbecue Sauce, any flavor

1 pkg. (6 oz.) **OSCAR MAYER** Grilled Chicken Breast Strips, chopped

2 Tbsp. **KRAFT** Light Ranch Reduced Fat Dressing

¼ cup chopped red bell pepper

¼ cup sliced green onions

1 Spread Neufchâtel cheese onto bottom of microwaveable 9-inch pie plate. Spread barbecue sauce over Neufchâtel cheese. Top with chicken.

2 Microwave on HIGH 2 min. or until heated through. Top with remaining ingredients.

3 Serve with WHEAT THINS Snack Crackers and cut up vegetables.

dips & appetizers

creamy coconut dip

prep: *5 min.*
plus refrigerating

makes: *48 servings,*
2 Tbsp. each.

1 pkg. (8 oz.) **PHILADELPHIA** Cream Cheese, softened

1 can (15 oz.) cream of coconut

1 tub (16 oz.) **COOL WHIP** Whipped Topping, thawed

1 Beat cream cheese and cream of coconut in large bowl with wire whisk until well blended.

2 Add whipped topping; gently stir until well blended. Cover. Refrigerate several hours or until chilled.

3 Serve with **HONEY MAID** Grahams Honey Sticks and cut-up fresh fruit.

dips & appetizers

sweet fruit dip

prep: *10 min.*
plus refrigerating

makes: *16 servings,*
2 Tbsp. each.

4 oz. (½ of 8-oz. pkg.) **PHILADELPHIA** Cream Cheese,
   softened

1 cup whole berry cranberry sauce

1 cup thawed **COOL WHIP** Whipped Topping

1 Beat cream cheese and cranberry sauce with electric mixer on medium speed until well blended. Gently stir in whipped topping; cover.

2 Refrigerate at least 1 hour or until ready to serve.

3 Serve with cut-up fresh fruit dippers.

dips & appetizers

heavenly ham roll-ups

prep: *15 min.*

bake: *20 min.*

makes: *15 servings,
1 roll-up each.*

1 pkg. (9 oz.) **OSCAR MAYER** Shaved Smoked Ham

5 Tbsp. **PHILADELPHIA** Light Cream Cheese Spread

15 asparagus spears (about 1 lb.), trimmed

1 Preheat oven to 350°F. Flatten ham slices; pat dry. Stack ham in piles of 2 slices each; spread each stack with 1 tsp. of the cream cheese spread.

2 Place 1 asparagus spear on one of the long sides of each ham stack; roll up. Place in 13×9-inch baking dish.

3 Bake 15 to 20 min. or until heated through.

dips & appetizers

creamy stuffed pastry bites

prep: *15 min.*

bake: *15 min.*

makes: *22 servings, 2 pastry bites each.*

4 oz. (½ of 8-oz. pkg.) **PHILADELPHIA** Cream Cheese, softened

½ cup finely chopped cooked turkey or chicken

2 green onions, sliced

½ tsp. chopped fresh parsley

   Salt and black pepper

1 pkg. (17¼ oz.) frozen puff pastry (2 sheets), thawed

1 egg

1 Tbsp. milk

1 Preheat oven to 400°F. Mix cream cheese, turkey, onions and parsley until well blended. Season with salt and pepper to taste.

2 Place pastry sheets on cutting board. Cut out 22 circles from each pastry sheet, using a 2-inch round cutter. Beat egg and milk with wire whisk until well blended.

3 Spoon 1 tsp. of the turkey mixture onto center of each pastry circle. Brush edge of pastry with egg mixture. Fold pastry in half to completely enclose filling; press edges together to seal. Place on baking sheet; brush tops with remaining egg mixture.

4 Bake 12 to 15 min. or until golden brown. Serve immediately.

dips & appetizers

party cheese ball

prep: *15 min.*
plus refrigerating

makes: *24 servings,*
2 Tbsp. each.

2 pkg. (8 oz. each) **PHILADELPHIA** Cream Cheese, softened

1 pkg. (8 oz.) **KRAFT** Shredded Sharp Cheddar Cheese

1 Tbsp. finely chopped onions

1 Tbsp. chopped red bell peppers

2 tsp. Worcestershire sauce

1 tsp. lemon juice

Dash ground red pepper (cayenne)

Dash salt

1 cup chopped **PLANTERS** Pecans

1 Beat cream cheese and Cheddar cheese in small bowl with electric mixer on medium speed until well blended.

2 Mix in all remaining ingredients except pecans; cover. Refrigerate several hours or overnight.

3 Shape into ball; roll in pecans. Serve with assorted **NABISCO** Crackers.

dips & appetizers

holiday cheese truffles

size-wise
Enjoy a single serving of this indulgent holiday treat.

special extra
Try these other coatings for these tasty truffles: sesame seeds, chopped fresh parsley, paprika and your favorite KRAFT Shredded Cheese.

variations
Prepare as directed, using one of the following options: Festive Wreath: Alternately arrange different flavored truffles in a large circle on platter to resemble a holiday wreath. Create a decorative bow out of green onion strips. Use to garnish wreath. Cheese Logs: Roll each half into 6-inch log. Roll in desired coatings as directed.

prep: *15 min.*

makes: *4 doz. truffles or 24 servings, 2 truffles and 5 crackers each.*

2 pkg. (8 oz. each) **PHILADELPHIA** Cream Cheese, softened

1 pkg. (8 oz.) **KRAFT** Shredded Sharp Cheddar Cheese

1 tsp. garlic powder

Dash ground red pepper (cayenne)

¼ cup chopped roasted red peppers

2 green onions, sliced

1⅔ cups **PLANTERS** Chopped Pecans

SOCIABLES Savory Crackers

1 Beat cream cheese, Cheddar cheese, garlic powder and ground red pepper with electric mixer until blended. Divide in half. Add roasted peppers to half and onions to other half; mix each until blended.

2 Refrigerate several hours or until chilled.

3 Shape into 24 (1-inch) balls. Roll in pecans. Refrigerate until ready to serve.

dips & appetizers

cheesy spinach and bacon dip

variation
Prepare as directed, using VELVEETA Made With 2% Milk Reduced Fat Pasteurized Prepared Cheese Product and PHILADELPHIA Neufchâtel Cheese, ⅓ Less Fat than Cream Cheese.

how to cut up VELVEETA
Cut VELVEETA (the whole loaf) into ½-inch-thick slices. Then, cut each slice crosswise in both directions to make cubes.

use your slow cooker
When serving this dip at a party, pour the prepared dip into a small slow cooker set on Low. This will keep the dip warm and at the ideal consistency for several hours. For best results, stir the dip occasionally to prevent hot spots.

prep: *10 min.*

makes: *4 cups or 32 servings, 2 Tbsp. each.*

1 pkg. (10 oz.) frozen chopped spinach, thawed, drained

1 lb. (16 oz.) **VELVEETA** Pasteurized Prepared Cheese Product, cut into ½-inch cubes

4 oz. (½ of 8-oz. pkg.) **PHILADELPHIA** Cream Cheese, cut up

1 can (10 oz.) **RO*TEL** Diced Tomatoes & Green Chilies, undrained

8 slices **OSCAR MAYER** Bacon, crisply cooked, drained and crumbled

1 Combine ingredients in microwaveable bowl.

2 Microwave on HIGH 5 min. or until **VELVEETA** is completely melted and mixture is well blended, stirring after 3 min.

Ro*Tel is a product of ConAgra Foods, Inc.

cream cheese nibbles

prep: *10 min.*
plus refrigerating

makes: *18 servings,*
2 pieces each.

1 pkg. (8 oz.) **PHILADELPHIA** Cream Cheese

½ cup **KRAFT** Sun-Dried Tomato Dressing

2 cloves garlic, sliced

3 small sprigs fresh rosemary, stems removed

6 sprigs fresh thyme, cut into pieces

1 tsp. black peppercorns

Peel of 1 lemon, cut into thin strips

1 Cut cream cheese into 36 pieces. Place in 9-inch pie plate.

2 Add remaining ingredients; toss lightly. Cover.

3 Refrigerate at least 1 hour or up to 24 hours. Serve with crusty bread, **NABISCO** Crackers or pita chips.

dips & appetizers

deviled ham finger sandwiches

make ahead
Prepare cream cheese mixture as directed. Cover and refrigerate up to 5 days. Spread onto bread slices and continue as directed. For easier spreading, mix 1 Tbsp. milk with chilled cream cheese mixture before spreading onto bread slices. Or prepare sandwiches as directed, but do not cut into quarters. Wrap in plastic wrap. Refrigerate until ready to serve. Cut into quarters just before serving.

substitute
Substitute MIRACLE WHIP Dressing for the mayo.

prep: *15 min.*

makes: *18 servings, 4 sandwich quarters each.*

1 pkg. (8 ounces) **PHILADELPHIA** Cream Cheese, softened

1 can (4.25 ounces) deviled ham

¼ cup **KRAFT** Mayo Real Mayonnaise

10 small stuffed green olives, finely chopped

36 slices white bread, crusts removed

1 Mix cream cheese, ham, mayo and olives until well blended.

2 Spread each of 18 of the bread slices with about 2 Tbsp. of the cream cheese mixture. Cover with remaining bread slices to make 18 sandwiches.

3 Cut each sandwich into quarters.

dips & appetizers

entrées & sides

Dishes made delicious with PHILADELPHIA Cream Cheese

zesty chicken pot pie
(recipe on page 216)

zesty chicken pot pie

serving suggestion
Serve with a mixed green salad and glass of fat-free milk.

make ahead
Prepare as directed except for baking. Wrap securely; freeze. When ready to bake, unwrap. Place strips of foil around edge to prevent over browning. Bake frozen pie at 425°F for 1 hour and 10 min. or until heated through.

substitutes
Prepare as directed, using PHILADELPHIA Neufchâtel Cheese, ⅓ Less Fat than Cream Cheese or GOOD SEASONS Zesty Italian Dressing or substituting turkey for the chicken.

prep: *20 min.*

bake: *25 min.*

makes: *8 servings.*

12 oz. (1½ pkg. [8 oz. each]) **PHILADELPHIA** Cream Cheese, cubed

½ cup chicken broth

3 cups chopped cooked chicken

2 pkg. (10 oz. each) frozen mixed vegetables, thawed

1 env. **GOOD SEASONS** Italian Salad Dressing & Recipe Mix

1 refrigerated ready-to-use refrigerated pie crust (½ of 15-oz. pkg.)

1 Preheat oven to 425°F. Place cream cheese in large saucepan. Add broth; cook on low heat until cream cheese is completely melted, stirring frequently with wire whisk. Stir in chicken, vegetables and salad dressing mix.

2 Spoon into 9-inch pie plate. Cover with pie crust; seal and flute edge. Cut several slits in crust to allow steam to escape. Place pie plate on baking sheet.

3 Bake 20 to 25 min. or until golden brown.

entrées & sides

chicken enchiladas

- 2 cups chopped cooked chicken or turkey
- 1 green bell pepper, chopped
- 4 oz. (½ of 8-oz. pkg.) **PHILADELPHIA** Cream Cheese, cubed
- ½ cup **TACO BELL**® **HOME ORIGINALS**® Thick 'N Chunky Salsa, divided
- 8 **TACO BELL**® **HOME ORIGINALS**® Flour Tortillas
- ¼ lb. (4 oz.) **VELVEETA** Pasteurized Prepared Cheese Product, cut into ½-inch cubes
- 1 Tbsp. milk

1 Preheat oven to 350°F. Mix chicken, green bell pepper, cream cheese and ¼ cup of the salsa in saucepan; cook on low heat until cream cheese is melted, stirring occasionally.

2 Spoon ⅓ cup of the chicken mixture down center of each tortilla; roll up. Place, seam-sides down, in lightly greased 13×9-inch baking dish. Place **VELVEETA** in small saucepan. Add milk; cook on low heat until **VELVEETA** is completely melted, stirring frequently. Pour over enchiladas; cover with foil.

3 Bake 20 min. or until heated through. Top with remaining ¼ cup salsa.

TACO BELL® and HOME ORIGINALS® are trademarks owned and licensed by Taco Bell Corp.

substitute
Prepare as directed, using PHILADELPHIA Neufchâtel Cheese, ⅓ Less Fat than Cream Cheese and VELVEETA Made With 2% Milk Reduced Fat Pasteurized Prepared Cheese Product.

shortcut
Substitute 1 pkg. (6 oz.) OSCAR MAYER Oven Roasted Chicken Breast Cuts for the chopped cooked fresh chicken.

prep: *20 min.*

bake: *20 min.*

makes: *4 servings, 2 enchiladas each.*

entrées & sides

bacon & tomato presto pasta

prep: *10 min.*

cook: *10 min.*

makes: *8 servings.*

8 slices **OSCAR MAYER** Bacon, chopped

½ cup cherry tomatoes

1 tub (8 oz.) **PHILADELPHIA** Chive & Onion Cream Cheese Spread

1 cup milk

½ cup **KRAFT** 100% Grated Parmesan Cheese

6 cups hot cooked penne pasta

1 Cook bacon in skillet 5 min. or until bacon is crisp, stirring occasionally. Drain skillet, leaving bacon in skillet. Stir in cherry tomatoes.

2 Add cream cheese spread, milk and Parmesan cheese; mix well. Cook until hot and bubbly, stirring frequently.

3 Stir in pasta.

entrées & sides

spaghetti with zesty bolognese

prep: *10 min.*

cook: *15 min.*

makes: *6 servings.*

1 small onion, chopped

¼ cup **KRAFT** Light Zesty Italian Reduced Fat Dressing

1 lb. extra lean ground beef

1 can (15 oz.) tomato sauce

1 can (14 oz.) diced tomatoes, undrained

2 Tbsp. **PHILADELPHIA** Neufchâtel Cheese, ⅓ Less Fat than Cream Cheese

12 oz. spaghetti, uncooked

¼ cup **KRAFT** 100% Grated Parmesan Cheese

1 Cook onions in dressing in large skillet on medium heat. Increase heat to medium-high. Add meat; cook, stirring frequently, until browned. Stir in tomato sauce and tomatoes. Bring to boil. Reduce heat to medium-low; simmer 15 min. Remove from heat. Stir in Neufchâtel cheese until well blended.

2 Meanwhile, cook pasta as directed on package.

3 Spoon sauce over pasta. Sprinkle with Parmesan cheese.

entrées & sides

creamy restaurant-style tortellini

prep: *5 min.*

cook: *15 min.*

makes: *6 servings, 1½ cups each.*

2 pkg. (9 oz. each) refrigerated three-cheese tortellini, uncooked

4 oz. (½ of 8-oz. pkg.) **PHILADELPHIA** Cream Cheese, cubed

1 cup milk

6 Tbsp. **KRAFT** 100% Grated Parmesan Cheese, divided

¼ tsp. black pepper

1 bag (6 oz.) baby spinach leaves

1 cup quartered cherry tomatoes (about ½ pint)

1 Cook tortellini as directed on package.

2 Meanwhile, place cream cheese in large skillet. Cook on low heat until cream cheese is melted, stirring occasionally. Whisk in milk gradually. Stir in 4 Tbsp. (¼ cup) of the Parmesan cheese and the black pepper. Add spinach; stir to coat. Drain pasta. Add to spinach mixture in skillet; mix lightly.

3 Sprinkle with tomatoes and remaining 2 Tbsp. Parmesan cheese just before serving.

entrées & sides

pasta primavera alfredo

prep: 5 min.

cook: 15 min.

makes: 5 servings,
1¼ cups each.

4 oz. (½ of 8-oz. pkg.) **PHILADELPHIA** Cream Cheese, cubed

¾ cup milk

½ cup **KRAFT** Shredded Parmesan Cheese

¼ cup (½ stick) butter or margarine

¼ tsp. white pepper

¼ tsp. garlic powder

⅛ tsp. ground nutmeg

2 cups small broccoli florets

1 cup chopped carrots

1 pkg. (9 oz.) refrigerated fettuccine

1 Place cream cheese, milk, Parmesan cheese and butter in small saucepan; cook on medium-low heat until cream cheese is completely melted and mixture is well blended, stirring occasionally. Add pepper, garlic powder and nutmeg; stir until well blended.

2 Meanwhile, add vegetables and pasta to 2½ qt. boiling water in large saucepan; cook 3 min. Drain.

3 Toss pasta mixture with the cream cheese mixture.

entrées & sides

italian five-cheese chicken roll-ups

prep: *10 min.*

cook: *35 min.*

makes: *4 servings.*

1 cup **KRAFT** Finely Shredded Italian* Five Cheese Blend, divided

2 oz. (¼ of 8-oz. pkg.) **PHILADELPHIA** Cream Cheese, softened

¼ cup finely chopped green bell peppers

½ tsp. dried oregano leaves

¼ tsp. garlic salt

4 small boneless, skinless chicken breast halves (1 lb.), pounded to ¼-inch thickness

1 cup spaghetti sauce

1 Preheat oven to 400°F. Mix ½ cup of the shredded cheese, the cream cheese, peppers, oregano and garlic salt until well blended. Shape into 4 logs. Place 1 log on one of the short ends of each chicken breast; press into chicken lightly. Roll up each chicken breast tightly, tucking in ends of chicken around filling to completely enclose filling.

2 Place, seam-sides down, in 13×9-inch baking dish sprayed with cooking spray. Spoon spaghetti sauce evenly over chicken; cover with foil.

3 Bake 30 min. or until chicken is cooked through (170°F). Remove foil; sprinkle chicken with remaining ½ cup shredded cheese. Bake an additional 3 to 5 min. or until cheese is melted.

*Made with quality cheeses crafted in the USA.

entrées & sides

stuffed fiesta burgers

prep: *15 min.*

grill: *9 min.*

makes: *4 servings,*
1 burger each.

1 lb. ground beef

1 pkg. (1¼ oz.) **TACO BELL**® **HOME ORIGINALS**® Taco
  Seasoning Mix

¼ cup **PHILADELPHIA** Chive & Onion Cream Cheese Spread

⅓ cup **KRAFT** Shredded Cheddar Cheese

4 hamburger buns, split, lightly toasted

½ cup **TACO BELL**® **HOME ORIGINALS**® Thick 'N Chunky
  Medium Salsa

1 avocado, peeled, pitted and cut into 8 slices

1 Preheat grill to medium heat. Mix meat and seasoning mix.
Shape into 8 thin patties. Mix cream cheese spread and shredded
cheese. Spoon about 2 Tbsp. of the cheese mixture onto center
of each of 4 of the patties; top with second patty. Pinch edges of
patties together to seal.

2 Grill 7 to 9 min. on each side or until cooked through (160°F).

3 Cover bottom halves of buns with burgers. Top with salsa,
avocado slices and top halves of buns.

TACO BELL® and HOME ORIGINALS® are trademarks owned and licensed by Taco
Bell Corp.

entrées & sides

parmesan-crusted chicken in cream sauce

prep: *15 min.*

cook: *15 min.*

makes: *4 servings.*

2 cups instant brown rice, uncooked

1 can (14 oz.) fat-free reduced-sodium chicken broth, divided

6 **RITZ** Crackers, finely crushed

2 Tbsp. **KRAFT** 100% Grated Parmesan Cheese

4 small boneless, skinless chicken breast halves (1 lb.)

2 tsp. oil

⅓ cup **PHILADELPHIA** Chive & Onion Light Cream Cheese Spread

¾ lb. asparagus spears, trimmed, steamed

1 Cook rice as directed on package, using 1¼ cups of the broth and ½ cup water.

2 Meanwhile, mix cracker crumbs and Parmesan cheese on plate. Rinse chicken with cold water; gently shake off excess water. Dip chicken in crumb mixture, turning each piece over to evenly coat both sides. Place in single layer in lightly greased shallow baking pan. Discard any remaining crumb mixture.

3 Heat oil in large nonstick skillet on medium heat. Add chicken; cook 5 to 6 min. on each side or until golden brown on both sides and cooked through (165°F). Place chicken on serving plate; cover to keep warm. Add remaining ½ cup broth and the cream cheese spread to skillet. Cook on medium heat just until mixture comes to boil, stirring constantly. Simmer 3 min. or until sauce is thickened, stirring frequently. Spoon sauce over chicken. Serve with the rice and asparagus.

entrées & sides

creamy roast beef sandwiches

prep: *5 min.*

cook: *15 min.*

makes: *6 servings,*
2 filled pita halves each.

1 cup sliced onions, separated into rings

1 Tbsp. butter or margarine

6 oz. (¾ of 8-oz. pkg.) **PHILADELPHIA** Cream Cheese, cubed

½ cup milk

1 Tbsp. **KRAFT** Prepared Horseradish

6 pita breads, cut in half

1 lb. shaved deli roast beef

2 medium tomatoes, chopped

2 cups shredded lettuce

1 Cook and stir onions in butter in medium skillet on medium heat until tender. Add cream cheese and milk; stir. Reduce heat to low; cook until cream cheese is completely melted and mixture is well blended, stirring occasionally. Stir in horseradish.

2 Fill pita pockets evenly with meat, tomatoes and lettuce.

3 Drizzle with the horseradish sauce.

entrées & sides

easy cauliflower & broccoli au gratin

prep: *10 min.*

cook: *13 min.*

makes: *10 servings, about ¾ cup each.*

 1 lb. large cauliflower florets

 1 lb. large broccoli florets

 ½ cup water

 4 oz. (½ of 8-oz. pkg.) **PHILADELPHIA** Cream Cheese, cubed

 ¼ cup milk

 ½ cup **BREAKSTONE'S** or **KNUDSEN** Sour Cream

1½ cups **KRAFT** Shredded Sharp Cheddar Cheese

10 **RITZ** Crackers, crushed

 3 Tbsp. **KRAFT** 100% Grated Parmesan Cheese

1 Place cauliflower and broccoli in 2-qt. microwaveable dish. Add water; cover. Microwave on HIGH 8 to 10 min. or until vegetables are tender; drain. Set aside.

2 Microwave cream cheese and milk in 2-cup microwaveable measuring cup or medium bowl 1 min. or until cream cheese is melted and mixture is well blended when stirred. Add sour cream; mix well. Pour over vegetables; sprinkle with Cheddar cheese. Microwave 2 min. or until cheese is melted.

3 Mix cracker crumbs and Parmesan cheese. Sprinkle over vegetables.

entrées & sides

family-favorite roast chicken

prep: *10 min.*

bake: *1 hour 30 min.*

makes: *8 servings.*

1 (4½-lb.) roasting chicken

¼ tsp. black pepper

⅛ tsp. salt

1 medium lemon, washed

4 oz. (½ of 8-oz. pkg.) **PHILADELPHIA** Cream Cheese, softened

1 Tbsp. Italian seasoning

½ cup **KRAFT** Zesty Italian Dressing

1 Preheat oven to 350°F. Rinse chicken; pat dry with paper towel. Use the tip of a sharp knife to separate the chicken skin from the meat in the chicken breast and tops of the legs. Sprinkle chicken both inside and out with the pepper and salt. Place in 13×9-inch baking dish.

2 Grate the lemon; mix the peel with cream cheese and Italian seasoning. Use a small spoon or your fingers to carefully stuff the cream cheese mixture under the chicken skin, pushing the cream cheese mixture carefully toward the legs, being careful to not tear the skin.

3 Cut the lemon in half; squeeze both halves into small bowl. Add dressing; beat with wire whisk until well blended. Drizzle evenly over chicken. Place the squeezed lemon halves inside the chicken cavity. Insert an ovenproof meat thermometer into thickest part of 1 of the chicken's thighs.

4 Bake 1 hour 30 min. or until chicken is no longer pink in center (165°F), basting occasionally with the pan juices.

entrées & sides

farmhouse chicken dinner

prep: *15 min.*

cook: *30 min.*

makes: *4 servings.*

¼ cup all-purpose flour

½ tsp. black pepper

4 small bone-in chicken breast halves (1½ lb.), skin removed

¼ cup **KRAFT** Light Zesty Italian Reduced Fat Dressing

2 cups baby carrots

1 onion, cut into wedges

1 can (14½ oz.) fat-free reduced-sodium chicken broth, divided

2 cups instant brown rice, uncooked

4 oz. (½ of 8-oz. pkg.) **PHILADELPHIA** Neufchâtel Cheese, ⅓ Less Fat than Cream Cheese, cubed

2 Tbsp. chopped fresh parsley

1 Mix flour and pepper in shallow dish. Add chicken; turn to evenly coat both sides of each piece with flour mixture. Gently shake off excess flour mixture; set aside. Heat dressing in large nonstick skillet on medium heat. Add chicken, meat-side down; cook 5 to 6 min. or until golden brown. Turn chicken; add carrots, onion and 1 cup of the broth. Cover. Reduce heat to medium-low; simmer 20 min. or until carrots are tender and chicken is cooked through (165°F).

2 Meanwhile, cook rice as directed on package. Spoon onto serving platter. Use slotted spoon to remove chicken and vegetables from skillet; place over rice. Cover to keep warm.

3 Add Neufchâtel cheese and remaining broth to skillet; increase heat to high. Cook until cheese is melted and sauce is well blended, stirring constantly. Reduce heat to medium-low; simmer 3 to 5 min. or until sauce is slightly thickened, stirring occasionally. Spoon over chicken and vegetables; sprinkle with parsley.

entrées & sides

20-minute skillet salmon

1 Tbsp. oil

4 salmon fillets (1 lb.)

1 cup fat-free milk

½ cup (½ of 8-oz. tub) **PHILADELPHIA** Light Cream Cheese Spread

½ cup chopped cucumbers

2 Tbsp. chopped fresh dill

1 Heat oil in large skillet on medium-high heat. Add salmon; cook 5 min. on each side or until salmon flakes easily with fork. Remove from skillet; cover to keep warm.

2 Add milk and cream cheese spread to skillet; cook and stir until cream cheese spread is melted and mixture is well blended. Stir in cucumbers and dill.

3 Return salmon to skillet. Cook 2 min. or until heated through. Serve salmon topped with the cream cheese sauce.

cooking know-how
When salmon is done, it will appear opaque and flake easily with fork.

food facts
Check salmon fillets for bones before cooking by running fingers over surface. Small bumps are usually a sign of bones. Use tweezers to remove any bones.

substitute
Substitute 2 tsp. dill weed for the 2 Tbsp. chopped fresh dill.

prep: *10 min.*

cook: *10 min.*

makes: *4 servings.*

diner special meatloaf

round out the meal
Serve with a steamed green vegetable, such as green beans, and a whole wheat roll.

great substitute
Substitute 1 pkg. (16 oz.) frozen LOUIS RICH Ground Turkey for the ground beef.

special extra
Garnish with chopped fresh chives just before serving.

prep time: *15 min.*

bake: *55 min.*

makes: *4 servings.*

1 lb. lean ground beef

½ cup **KRAFT** Original Barbecue Sauce

½ cup dry bread crumbs

1 egg, lightly beaten

1¼ cups water

¾ cup milk

2 Tbsp. butter or margarine

½ tsp. salt

1½ cups instant potato flakes

3 oz. **PHILADELPHIA** Cream Cheese, cubed

2 **KRAFT** Singles

1 Preheat oven to 375°F. Mix meat, barbecue sauce, bread crumbs and egg. Shape into loaf in 12×8-inch baking dish.

2 Bake 55 minutes. Meanwhile, bring water to boil in medium saucepan. Add milk, butter and salt; stir in potato flakes. Add cream cheese; stir until completely melted.

3 Spread potato mixture over meatloaf; top with Singles. Bake an additional 5 minutes or until Singles begin to melt.

entrées & sides

creamy bow-tie pasta with chicken and broccoli

prep: *10 min.*

cook: *15 min.*

makes: *6 servings, about 1½ cups each.*

3 cups (8 oz.) farfalle (bow-tie pasta), uncooked

4 cups broccoli florets

3 Tbsp. **KRAFT** Roasted Red Pepper Italian with Parmesan Dressing

6 small boneless, skinless chicken breast halves (1½ lb.)

2 cloves garlic, minced

2 cups tomato-basil spaghetti sauce

4 oz. (½ of 8-oz. pkg.) **PHILADELPHIA** Neufchâtel Cheese, ⅓ Less Fat than Cream Cheese, cubed

¼ cup **KRAFT** 100% Grated Parmesan Cheese

1 Cook pasta as directed on package, adding broccoli to the cooking water for the last 3 min. of the pasta cooking time. Meanwhile, heat dressing in large nonstick skillet on medium heat. Add chicken and garlic; cook 5 min. Turn chicken over; continue cooking 4 to 5 min. or until chicken is cooked through (170°F).

2 Drain pasta mixture in colander; return to pan and set aside. Add spaghetti sauce and Neufchâtel cheese to chicken in skillet; cook on medium-low heat 2 to 3 min. or until Neufchâtel cheese is completely melted, mixture is well blended and chicken is coated with sauce, stirring occasionally. Remove chicken from skillet; keep warm. Add sauce mixture to pasta mixture; mix well. Transfer to six serving bowls.

3 Cut chicken crosswise into thick slices; fan out chicken over pasta mixture. Sprinkle evenly with Parmesan cheese.

entrées & sides

chive & onion mashed potatoes

2 lb. potatoes, peeled, quartered (about 6 cups)

½ cup milk

1 tub (8 oz.) **PHILADELPHIA** Chive & Onion Cream Cheese Spread

¼ cup **KRAFT** Ranch Dressing

1 Place potatoes and enough water to cover in 3-qt. saucepan. Bring to boil.

2 Reduce heat to medium; cook 20 to 25 min. or until tender. Drain.

3 Mash potatoes, gradually stirring in milk, cream cheese spread and dressing until light and fluffy. Serve immediately.

make ahead

Mix ingredients as directed; spoon into 1½-qt. casserole dish. Cover. Refrigerate several hours or overnight. When ready to serve, bake, uncovered, at 350°F 1 hour or until heated through.

substitute

Substitute KRAFT Three Cheese Ranch Dressing for Ranch Dressing.

prep: *10 min.*

cook: *25 min.*

makes: *10 servings, ½ cup each.*

entrées & sides

index

index

DESSERTS

DIPS

ENTRÉES

index

index

METRIC CONVERSION CHART

VOLUME MEASUREMENTS (dry)

⅛ teaspoon = 0.5 mL
¼ teaspoon = 1 mL
½ teaspoon = 2 mL
¾ teaspoon = 4 mL
1 teaspoon = 5 mL
1 tablespoon = 15 mL
2 tablespoons = 30 mL
¼ cup = 60 mL
⅓ cup = 75 mL
½ cup = 125 mL
⅔ cup = 150 mL
¾ cup = 175 mL
1 cup = 250 mL
2 cups = 1 pint = 500 mL
3 cups = 750 mL
4 cups = 1 quart = 1 L

VOLUME MEASUREMENTS (fluid)

1 fluid ounce (2 tablespoons) = 30 mL
4 fluid ounces (½ cup) = 125 mL
8 fluid ounces (1 cup) = 250 mL
12 fluid ounces (1½ cups) = 375 mL
16 fluid ounces (2 cups) = 500 mL

WEIGHTS (mass)

½ ounce = 15 g
1 ounce = 30 g
3 ounces = 90 g
4 ounces = 120 g
8 ounces = 225 g
10 ounces = 285 g
12 ounces = 360 g
16 ounces = 1 pound = 450 g

DIMENSIONS

1/16 inch = 2 mm
⅛ inch = 3 mm
¼ inch = 6 mm
½ inch = 1.5 cm
¾ inch = 2 cm
1 inch = 2.5 cm

OVEN TEMPERATURES

250°F = 120°C
275°F = 140°C
300°F = 150°C
325°F = 160°C
350°F = 180°C
375°F = 190°C
400°F = 200°C
425°F = 220°C
450°F = 230°C

BAKING PAN SIZES

Utensil	Size in Inches/Quarts	Metric Volume	Size in Centimeters
Baking or Cake Pan (square or rectangular)	8×8×2	2 L	20×20×5
	9×9×2	2.5 L	23×23×5
	12×8×2	3 L	30×20×5
	13×9×2	3.5 L	33×23×5
Loaf Pan	8×4×3	1.5 L	20×10×7
	9×5×3	2 L	23×13×7
Round Layer Cake Pan	8×1½	1.2 L	20×4
	9×1½	1.5 L	23×4
Pie Plate	8×1¼	750 mL	20×3
	9×1¼	1 L	23×3
Baking Dish or Casserole	1 quart	1 L	—
	1½ quarts	1.5 L	—
	2 quarts	2 L	—